PR IN PRACTICE SERIES

Planning and Managing Public Relations Campaigns

Second Edition

Anne Gregory

CHARTERED INSTITUTE OF PUBLIC RELATIONS

KOGAN PAGE

London and Philadelphia

*To Mark, for his patient listening, sound counsel
and several late nights.*

First published as *Planning and Managing a Public Relation Campaign* in 1996
Reprinted in 1997, 1998, 1999 and 2000
Second edition published in 2000
Reprinted in 2002, 2003, 2004, 2005, 2006, 2008

Kogan Page Limited
120 Pentonville Road
London N1 9JN
United Kingdom
www.kogan-page.co.uk

Kogan Page US
525 South 4th Street, #241
Philadelphia PA 19147
USA

British Library Cataloguing in Publication Data

A CIP record for this book is available from the British Library.

ISBN-10 0 7494 2991 7
ISBN-13 978 0 7494 2991 1

Typeset by Jean Cussons Typesetting, Diss, Norfolk
Printed and bound in India by Replika Press Pvt Ltd

Contents

Acknowledgements   *vi*
About the author   *viii*

1 Planning and managing can be fun!   **1**
  Everyone can plan and manage   1
  Planning in public relations   2
  The role of public relations in business   5
  The role of the public relations professional within
  organisations   7
  Organising for action   14
  Who does what in public relations?   17

2 Public relations in context   **20**
  Context is vitally important   20
  Publics   21
  Sectoral considerations   24
  Organisational development – business stage   25

	Organisational characteristics	28
	Issues	30
	Public opinion	31
	Timescales	32
	Resources	33
3	**Starting the planning process**	**34**
	Getting in control	34
	Why planning is important	35
	Public relations policy	37
	Basic questions in planning	39
	The 10 stages of planning	43
4	**Analysis**	**48**
	The first planning step	48
	PEST analysis	49
	Spotting the issues	53
	SWOT analysis	56
	What state the stakeholder?	57
	Who should undertake the research?	60
	Research techniques	61
	Investment in research pays – two cases in point	68
5	**Setting objectives**	**78**
	Knowing where you're going	78
	Attitude is all important	79
	The communication chain	81
	Communicating on the Internet	87
	How 'receivers' use information	91
	Setting realistic objectives	93
	Eight golden rules of objective setting	95
	Constraints on objectives	97
	Strategic and tactical objectives	98
6	**Knowing the publics and messages**	**100**
	Who shall we talk to and what shall we say?	100
	What is public opinion?	101

Types of public 104
So what about the media? 109
The implications for targeting publics 110
How to select your publics 110
What shall we say? 112
Determining the messages 113
How the message should be presented 114

7 Strategy and tactics **117**
Getting the strategy right 117
What is strategy? 118
From strategy to tactics 119
What tactics should you employ? 121
Different campaigns need different tactics 125
Sustaining long-term programmes 139
The big 'What if?' – contingency planning 144

8 Timescales and resources **147**
Timescales 147
Critical path analysis 149
Longer-term plans 150
Resources 155

9 Knowing what you've achieved: evaluation and review **162**
Measuring success 162
The benefits of evaluation 164
Why practitioners don't evaluate 165
Principles of evaluation 168
An evaluation model and some other measures 171
Media analysis 175
Reviewing the situation 178
Help, the strategy's not working! 179
External and internal review drivers 180
And finally! 182

Index *183*

Acknowledgements

In drawing up a list of those organisations and individuals who must be thanked for helping with the writing of this book, it is very difficult to know where to start.

First of all there are all the organisations I have worked for and with whom over the years I have built up my knowledge and experience of public relations to an extent where this book was possible.

Then there are those who have generously supplied me with materials, including the Institute of Public Relations (I have borrowed shamelessly from their Excellence Awards), Pilkington PLC, Lansons Communications, Echo Research, Firefly Communications, Manning, Selvage and Lee, and Shandwick. Thanks go to Professor Tim Traverse-Healy and the Distance Learning Programme at Stirling University for permission to use ideas taken from materials prepared by Ann Dunne, Sam Black, Danny Moss, Don Bathie and George Panigyrakis.

I would like to thank the public relations students at Leeds Metropolitan University for whom I prepare materials on planning and managing public relations, and who constantly stimulate my thinking

I am very grateful to the University for giving me dedicated time to prepare this new edition and to Sue Hall, who did the final word-processing for me.

To the CIPR/Kogan Page Editorial Board, many thanks for your encouragement and support.

About the author

Anne Gregory is Head of the School of Business Strategy and an assistant dean of Leeds Business School, a Faculty of Leeds Metropolitan University.

Before entering academic life in 1991 she spent 10 years in public relations at a senior level both in-house and in consultancy.

At Leeds Metropolitan University Anne ran the undergraduate public relations course between 1991 to 1995 on which she still teaches. She maintains a lively interest in public relations practice and is regularly involved in consultancy work. She is a non-executive director of Bradford Community Health Trust with a special interest in communication issues.

As chair of the Chartered Institute of Public Relations (CIPR) Education and Training Committee, Anne initiated the CIPR/Kogan Page series of books on public relations and is its consultant editor. She is also the author of several articles about leading-edge public relations practice.

1

Planning and managing can be fun!

EVERYONE CAN PLAN AND MANAGE

Mention the words 'planning' or 'managing' to some people, particularly if they are creative, and they are immediately struck with horror.

On the other hand, some 'management types' like to surround the words with a great mystique. Only certain kinds of people are capable of doing such lofty activities and most of us have to be content with carrying out the instructions of those who know about these things.

This is rubbish! Everyone is capable of planning and managing – we all do it all the time. We plan our home lives –

what to eat and when, especially if we're having friends round. We plan holidays, how to spend Christmas, how to make large purchases and how to manage the conflicting demands of various members of the family whether they live with us or not.

Work and social life demand planning to a greater or lesser extent. Sometimes this planning is formal; sometimes it's just a pattern we follow when we repeat a familiar task. Certainly if we want to be in charge of our lives, and given the pace of change and activity, we need to plan to fit everything in and give ourselves space to have some fun.

And that is at the heart of planning and management. We don't do it to make our lives over-regulated and predictable, we do it to ensure everything is done that needs to be done, to create space and to put us in control. We drive events instead of being driven by them.

Planning and managing things properly can be exciting. It's a creative process. It's a process that stimulates our intellect, can bring great satisfaction and, by harnessing various techniques, can ensure we are more effective and efficient in the way we work.

PLANNING IN PUBLIC RELATIONS

A good starting point when thinking about public relations and planning is to look at some of the recent definitions of public relations. According to the UK's Institute of Public Relations:

> Public relations practice is the <u>planned</u> and <u>sustained</u> effort to <u>establish</u> and <u>maintain</u> goodwill and mutual understanding between an organisation and its publics.

At the heart of this definition is the notion that public relations has to be planned. It is a deliberate, carefully thought-out process. It also requires ongoing (sustained) activity that is not haphazard. The activity is concerned with initiating (establishing) and maintaining a process of mutual understanding. In other words it involves a dialogue where an organisation and its various publics seek to listen to each other and understand each other. This will usually result in some change or action by the parties involved.

Implicit in all this is that public relations practitioners carefully consider how programmes need to begin, and continue in a structured way to the benefit both of their organisation and to the 'publics' their organisation interacts with.

More recent definitions by the IPR state that:

> Public relations is about reputation – the result of what you do, what you say and what others say about you.

and

> Public relations practice is the discipline which looks after reputation with the aim of earning understanding and support and influencing opinion and behaviour.

A good reputation is not something that is earned overnight. It has to be carefully and considerately cultivated. It is something that is earned over a period of time as understanding and support develop for an organisation. The management of reputation has to be meticulously undertaken with integrity and honesty. It is something that is very fragile and can be lost quickly if words or actions are found to be out of sympathy with reality, or if careless talk gets out of hand. There is no better example of that than Gerald Ratner's comments about the jewellery in his chain of shops being 'crap'.

On the other hand the careful handling by IBM and The Body Shop of their reputations means that they have enjoyed public esteem for many years. The reality of their spoken, public claims is borne out by their actual products and services.

A virtuous circle is created where a good reputation raises

expectations about the kind of products or services a company supplies and the quality of the products or services enhances the reputation.

Public relations has a job of work to do

All this means that public relations has a real job of work to do. It has to contribute directly to business success. If its task is guarding and managing reputation and relationships this must have a demonstrable effect, and not just result in a 'feel-good' factor. Spending money on establishing a dialogue with key publics and building a reputation has to result in tangible benefits to the organisation. Publics are influenced in their favour.

If a company has a good reputation the evidence is that people are more likely to:

- try its new products;
- buy its shares;
- believe its advertising;
- want to work for it;
- do business with it when all other things are equal;
- support it in difficult times;
- give it a higher financial value.

Establishing and maintaining a good reputation with key publics is a meticulous, time- and energy-consuming business, requiring all the skills and attributes of planners and managers of the highest calibre. To be involved with building the reputation of a company is quite an awesome task.

THE ROLE OF PUBLIC RELATIONS IN BUSINESS

To understand how public relations programmes and campaigns are planned and managed, it is first essential to understand the role of public relations in business.

It is not the aim of this book to go into the detail of how organisations are structured and managed, and how they function. There are many excellent textbooks on this. It is, however, incumbent on all public relations practitioners to understand these issues; otherwise they will not be able to fulfil their proper role within their organisation and certainly will not be able to operate as senior managers.

Simply put, an organisation consists of three elements:

- fixed assets such as its buildings, office furniture, car fleet and products;
- liquid assets or the money which lubricates the business;
- people.

Its fixed assets have a finite value and can be accounted for on a balance sheet. Similarly, the amount of liquid assets an organisation has can be measured. It is obvious that the number of people that work for an organisation can be counted, but in many ways employees are an unquantifiable asset. Their capabilities are basically unbounded. They are the ones who put life into an organisation to create added value. They are the ones who use their creativity and ingenuity to design new products and sell them. They provide the customer service. They make organisations work. Assets, whether fixed or liquid, on their own are neutral commodities.

Furthermore, people interact with other people who are not necessarily a part of the organisation. They create customer relationships, they have families and friends who may or who may not support their organisation. They deal with suppliers, with local and central government, with the local community and so on.

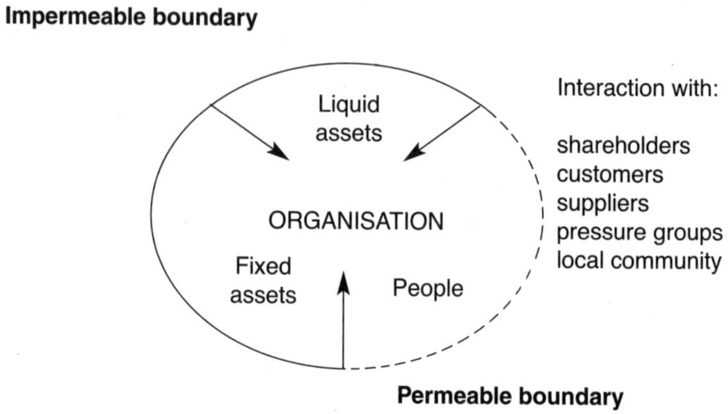

Impermeable boundary

Figure 1.1 *How people extend the boundaries of an organisation*

People are an infinitely expandable resource and they blur the edges of an organisation's boundaries by drawing into the organisation other people, who strictly speaking are external to its operation. Furthermore, some employees are also members of groups external to the organisation, but critical to its success. As well as being employees, they can be customers, shareholders, and are probably members of the local community.

The main role of the chief executive of an organisation is to provide vision. He or she should have vision not only of how to do things well now, but most importantly for the future direction of the organisation. Badly managed organisations have no clear direction. They have no clear long-term objectives, but stumble along being constantly diverted to deal with the crises or apparent opportunities of the day without being focused on achieving their main, long-term objectives.

THE ROLE OF THE PUBLIC RELATIONS PROFESSIONAL WITHIN ORGANISATIONS

An organisation's strategy (which determines long-term direction and scope) is determined after a great deal of analysis and decision-making. Many people, both outside and inside the organisation, will contribute to this process. Having developed a strategy, this will need to be communicated so that it can be supported and implemented. Public relations has an essential role to play in this process, both in helping to develop the strategy itself and in its communication.

Communication is intelligence

The job of the public relations professional is to communicate with and build relationships with all the organisation's publics. They are (or should be) acutely aware of the environment in which the organisation operates. This is vital because publics exist within that environment and it is not possible to understand people fully unless there is a clear appreciation of the social, technological, economic, political and cultural issues and factors that influence them and drive their lives. Public relations professionals, along with other colleagues, can supply that intelligence to the strategic planners. Thus they can be seen to have a 'boundary-spanning' role. They operate at the edge of the organisation, bridging the gap between it and its external publics. They have one foot in the organisation and one foot outside. Being able to represent the views of the external publics, and their likely reactions to decisions, is a vital perspective that public relations professionals can bring to strategic planning. Furthermore, public relations professionals are also usually the communication managers within organisations and can draw information together about an organisation's internal publics.

Of course information about the specifics of contextual factors, for example economic and financial facts, and intelligence about technological developments, will also be provided by specialists scattered throughout the organisation. The public relations function, because of its 'boundary-spanning role', can act as a central intelligence-gathering function and, provided there are suitably trained individuals, supply an analysis and interpretation service too. Public relations can contribute its detailed knowledge of publics and ensure that the views and attitudes of those stakeholders who hold the well-being of the organisation in their hands are taken into account.

This strategic use of the public relations function implies that there is a recognition of its status by management. Public relations is more than a tactical tool used purely to 'communicate' information or add a gloss to information. It is an integral part of the strategic development process grounded on thorough-going research and skilled, objective analysis.

Some of the specialist contacts that the public relations function have are invaluable sources of early information and can pinpoint emerging issues that may have profound impact on an organisation. For example, media content analysis can identify the importance of an issue or the direction that public opinion is likely to take on an issue. Public affairs contacts can flag up government thinking on prospective legislation and City contacts can give early warning of likely investor activity.

Being able to make sense of the environment, public relations professionals not only provide intelligence to the strategic development process, but contribute to the general decision-making within organisations. Because they have antennae that are alert to the external and internal environment that the organisation operates within, they can bring an invaluable, independent perspective to decision-making by managers' who are often too close to a situation to act objectively, or who are unaware of some of the ramifications of those decisions as far as the outside world is concerned. It could well be that what on the face of it appears to be correct business decisions have to be questioned when they are set within a broader context. For example, it might make apparent business sense for an organisation to obtain supplies from the cheapest, most reliable source. But what if that source employs child labour?

There is therefore a two-fold role for the public relations professional here. First, it is to keep senior management informed of what is happening in the social environment, which is peopled by its stakeholders, so that this is taken into account as decisions are made. The communication process is two-way as Figure 1.2 shows.

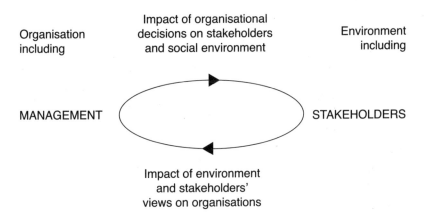

Organisation including

Impact of organisational decisions on stakeholders and social environment

Environment including

MANAGEMENT

STAKEHOLDERS

Impact of environment and stakeholders' views on organisations

Figure 1.2 *The two-way information flow between an organisation and its environment*

Second, it is to counsel management on the implications of its decisions, taking into account the likely reaction of key publics who directly affect the well-being or otherwise of a company. The public relations professional is the monitor of public opinion, and the conscience and ethical mentor of the organisation.

Communication skill

Once strategy is determined, it needs to be communicated. Public relations professionals can be used by senior management to advise on both the content of the communication itself and the mechanics to be used for relaying information to publics and back from them. Because strategic information and plans are so important, management are often tempted to communicate them in pompous language and in an inappropriate form, for example a highly glossy brochure that permits no discussion or questioning! The communication professional must resist such actions and provide skilled advice on how to undertake the communication task.

The very process of insisting that clear messages are relayed to important groups of people helps to put rigour into strategic thinking and decision-making. It helps to clear woolly, unrealistic aspirations and forces management to think through the practical implications of their planning. It is possible to cloak reality behind fine-sounding words. Distilling ideas down to simple language provides a check on how realistic those ideas are and makes comparisons between what's said and what's done more simple. So, if the reality doesn't meet the claim, don't say it!

At a tactical level, the role of the public relations practitioner is to manage appropriate communication between an organisation and its stakeholders and vice versa by ensuring that both the content and the technique are suitable and timely.

For example, shareholders will want to know about the future development plans of a company in some detail, including its overseas aspirations. How and when that information is relayed to them is very important. UK customers, on the other hand, are less likely to be so concerned about this. They will first want to know that a particular shop will be open next week or that a favourite product will continue to be available. The fact that the company plans to open outlets in Hong Kong or Singapore in 2005 will probably not concern them, unless of course they are shareholders too.

The importance of communication

So why is communication important?

First of all it helps to further the strategic objectives of an organisation because it seeks to enlist the support of all the various groups or key publics by ensuring the vision and values of the chief executive and organisation are clearly communicated. The point of the communication is not just passing on information about the vision, but to gain active pursuit of or at least assent to those objectives (depending on the public). The communication is designed to influence behaviour.

Of course, if the organisation listens as well as speaks and acts, its communication will have been affected by research undertaken with those key publics and will continue to be affected by them. It is, therefore, more likely to be effective in its communication, as it is not likely to say and do things that are out of step with the views of its stakeholders.

Second it positively fosters relationships with key publics. These publics are ultimately responsible for the destiny of the organisation for good or ill. As a result of this, good communication enhances the opportunities that are presented to organisations by both identifying them early and facilitating the actions that are required to capitalise on them (whether this be a sales opportunity or an opportunity to influence legislation). It also helps minimise the threats by spotting problems or potential conflicts early (for example, identifying increasing employee disquiet or discontent with a proposed company action).

The position of public relations within organisations

More detailed information on the role of public relations practitioners is given in Chapter 2. At this stage it is important to look at the position and status that public relations occupies within organisations, since that is linked to its role as a strategic or tactical function.

A good indication of how public relations is regarded is to establish where the function is placed. If senior public relations managers are part of the 'dominant coalition'[1] of company decision-makers, then public relations is likely to serve a key strategic role. Those individuals are likely to undertake the research and counselling activities already outlined. If not, public relations is likely to be largely tactical. It could well be seen just as a part of the marketing communications mix or regarded as largely to do with presenting information about the organisation in an acceptable (usually to the organisation) way, ie as propaganda or spin.

Another indication of how seriously the activity is taken is to gauge whether it is mainly reactive or proactive. Of course there is always a level of reactive public relations in any programme. However good the planning, the unexpected is likely to occur, whether that be a pressure group making an unexpected attack (justified or ill-founded) or another organisation making a takeover bid out of the blue. There are also opportunistic openings that should be grasped. It might be, for example, that there is an interest in the media over famine in Africa. If your organisation is a charity helping orphaned African children you would be provided with a golden opportunity to publicise your own work.

In organisations where public relations is taken seriously and proactively, it is normally found that the senior practitioner holds a major position in the organisation. He or she

---

[1]From Grunig, J E and Hunt, T (1984) *Managing Public Relations*, Holt, Rinehart and Winston, New York

will provide a counselling role for fellow senior managers and directors and will have overall responsibility for the communication strategy of the organisation – that might include determining the key overall marketing, advertising and promotional strategy. It will certainly involve working very closely with those disciplines.

Activity will be directed at building reputation positively and will have a strategic purpose. Issues like social responsibility and corporate governance will be taken seriously. Programmes will be based on careful formal and informal research, and a knowledge of who the key publics are, how these publics regard the organisation and what they see as priorities. Communication with the publics will be two-way, with the organisation being willing to change as required as a result. The programmes that are devised will be concerned with impact, and aim to influence attitudes, opinions and behaviours. They will not be obsessed with process such as how many news releases are produced, but the effectiveness of public relations activity will be closely monitored. Often these organisations will be industry leaders and setting the pace in the market. They will usually be the ones available to the media and seen to be the voice of their industry. They are the wholly open, communicative organisations.

In organisations where public relations is seen as a lower order activity and where its practice is normally reactive, certain telltale traits will be evident. The practitioner will not hold a senior management role and will not be involved in corporate decision-making. The task will be to respond to events and will often be defensive. The function will tend to communicate what has already happened, and the activity will be largely one-way, with the organisation telling the world what it has done or is doing and not being influenced by what the world is saying to it. Any progress will be an evolution of what has happened in the past. The practitioner will not feel valued or in control and will not be a part of the 'dominant coalition'.

It is partly the public relations industry and individual practitioners who have encouraged this reactive, technical role for public relations. Too often public relations has been regarded as just media relations – free media publicity at that – or as just a part of marketing communication. The schematic in Figure 1.3 shows the relationship between public relations and marketing, and indicates the shared areas of activity and those areas where public relations has a quite separate remit.

Public relations practitioners also have only themselves to blame for not learning as much as they should about business and how it operates. How can they be at the decision-making table if they have no real grasp on what makes a business tick?

In surveys, lack of financial and budgeting skills were perceived as being the greatest deficiency in public relations practitioners. Other deficiencies were problem-solving and decision-making, goal-setting and prioritising, planning and organisation, analytical skills and time management.

To mature fully as a discipline, public relations must take on the responsibilities of knowledge, planning and management just as any other business function. For example, being able to read a balance sheet and knowing how to undertake research are basic requirements.

ORGANISING FOR ACTION

Another book in this series, *Running a Public Relations Department*, looks in detail at how the public relations function should be organised. However, this is covered briefly here to provide an indication of the main things to be considered.

The way the public relations operation is usually organised is to split it along either task or functional lines. Single operators, however, have to do everything!

Some organisations have a task-oriented structure, that is,

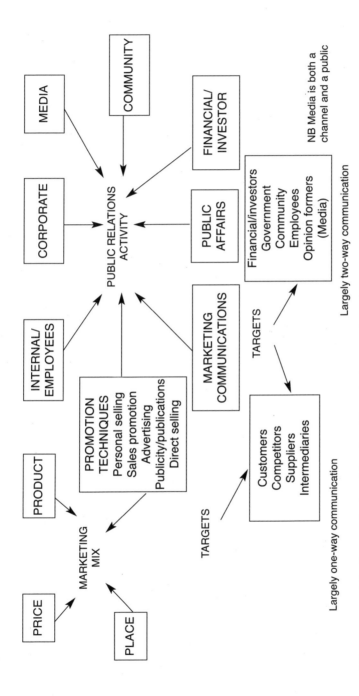

Figure 1.3 *The inter-relationship of public relations and marketing*

the individual jobs or tasks are separated out and given to small groups or individuals to perform. Thus the structure may be as follows:

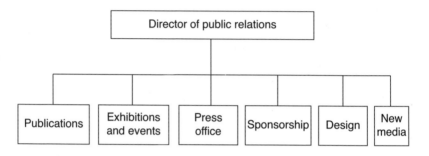

Other organisations split on functional lines. That is, the areas of activity are separated out and groups or individuals tackle all the tasks. A functional structure may look something like this:

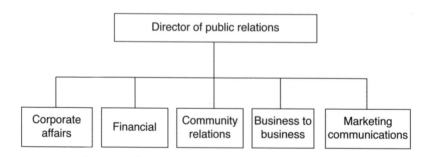

Where public relations is conducted for a company that is split into separate operating companies, sometimes with different names, the situation is infinitely more variable. Some groups have very large corporate departments which undertake activity for the group as a whole and for all the operating companies. In other groups there is a very small corporate operation dealing with major corporate activities such as financial and government affairs, and maybe corporate sponsorship. The rest of the activity is then devolved to the operating companies. Normally the operating pattern that applies in the business as a whole also applies to public relations activity, that is, if business is very much controlled from the centre then public relations is likely to be controlled from the centre also. On the other hand, if the approach is to let the operating companies function as virtually autonomous units, then that is also likely to be the approach for public relations.

WHO DOES WHAT IN PUBLIC RELATIONS?

In their seminal work on public relations, James Grunig and Todd Hunt[1] refer to work spearheaded by Glen Broom and David Dozier in which two dominant public relations roles were identified.

- *The communication technician.* Who is not involved in making organisational decisions but who carries out public relations programmes such as writing press releases, editing house magazines and designing Web pages. This person is probably not too involved in undertaking research or evaluating programmes; he or she is concerned primarily with implementation.
- *The communication manager.* Who plans and manages public relations programmes, counsels management, makes communication policy decisions and so on.

Within this second category, there are three main types of manager role.

[1]Grunig, J E and Hunt, T (1984) *Managing Public Relations*, Holt, Rinehart and Winston, New York.

- *The expert prescriber.* Who researches and defines public relations problems, develops programmes and implements them, maybe with the assistance of others.
- *The communication facilitator.* Who acts as a go-between, keeping two-way communication between an organisation and its publics. He or she is a liaison person, interpreter and mediator.
- *The problem-solving process facilitator.* Who helps others in the organisation solve their public relations problems. This person acts as a sort of counsellor/adviser on the planning and implementation of programmes. (This is a role often fulfilled by specialist consultancies.)

David Dozier also identifies two middle-level roles that sit between the manager and the technician role.

- *Media relations role.* This is a two-way function where the individual keeps the media informed, and informs the organisation of the needs and concerns of the media. This is not just the production and dissemination of messages from the organisation to the media, but a highly skilled role requiring detailed knowledge and a profound understanding of the media. It is often fulfilled by someone who has made the crossover from journalism to public relations. It also goes some way to explaining why, if a former journalist is employed to undertake public relations, the function remains focused on media relations.
- *Communication and liaison role.* Serves higher-level public relations managers by representing the organisation at events and meetings, and positively creating opportunities for management to communicate with internal and external publics.

The broad technician and manager roles vary from organisation to organisation. At the lower level, in large organisation split on task lines, a technician may only write for the house journal. In other organisations he or she may do several other writing jobs too, such as preparing speeches, especially if the department is functional in orientation or if it is small.

At the middle level, practitioners may be responsible for a whole press relations programme or undertake employee relations only. They may be involved in both. Some may specialise in research or planning and have little to do with implementation, or they may be an account executive in a consultancy who has to turn a hand to a whole range of planning and implementation tasks.

At higher levels, public relations managers plan whole programmes and counsel senior management on policy, as well as supervise middle- and lower-level practitioners.

In practice most public relations activities require a mixture of technician and manager roles. Many managers hold a number of the management roles indicated either at the same time, or at various stages in their careers, and not many people, at this stage of the profession's growth, are entirely removed from the implementation role.

The growing complexity of the issues that public relations practitioners are being asked to handle is leading to increasing specialisation in some areas. At the simplest level this is demonstrated by the fact that many consultancies now bill themselves as specialists in, for example, fashion or personality or hi-tech public relations and the larger, one-stop agencies have for a long time had quite discrete specialist functions within them, such as public affairs or consumer divisions.

2

Public relations in context

CONTEXT IS VITALLY IMPORTANT

To plan and manage campaigns effectively it is vitally important to look at the context in which public relations activity
takes place, since this differs from organisation to organisation. It helps to look at the factors affecting organisations in a
systematic way, and addressing the areas outlined in Figure
2.1 provides a blueprint for doing this.

This research is not about specific public relations problems
or opportunities (more of this in Chapter 3), but it is vital
background information required in order to plan and
manage effectively.

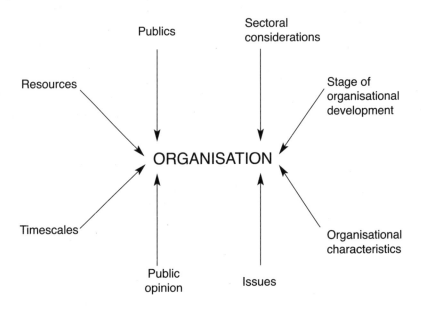

Figure 2.1 *Factors to be considered when researching the background for public relations activity*

PUBLICS

Chapter 6 has a much more detailed discussion of publics, but from the outset it is important that the public relations practitioner is aware of the whole range of publics that must be communicated with. This will be a major factor in deciding the public relations task. Each public will have a different communication requirement, although the information given to each must not conflict.

The object of the exercise is to enlist the support of these publics. Sometimes that support will need to be very active and immediate, for example, you want customers to buy your products and shareholders to support your company activities by not selling their shares. Sometimes the support is less active and not bound by specific timescales. For example, you might organise a community relations campaign, simply because you feel it right to put something back into a community that provides most of your workforce. There might be no specific business objectives, but the feeling of goodwill that the campaign engenders may make recruitment easier or minimise the possibility of objections being raised if you want to extend your factory in the future. Having undertaken a longer-term, goodwill-building programme you can, if you need to, switch more easily to a focused programme which seeks to enlist active support.

With some publics you might want to change opinions and behaviour, with others you might want to confirm existing behaviour or opinions, and yet with others you might want to engender an opinion or pattern of behaviour where previously that public was entirely neutral.

Factors to bear in mind when considering publics include the following:

- *Range.* That is the breadth of publics concerned. For some organisations, for example, manufacturers of highly specialised military components, the range of publics may be very small. For other organisations, for instance, the Department of Health, the range of publics is very large indeed.
- *Numbers and location.* Some organisations have a range of publics that fall into large uniform blocks, for example, the multiple retailers will have large groups of customers, suppliers and local authorities as some of their audiences. Others, for example project engineers, will have a whole range of publics, often small in number, attached to each project. Some organisations have publics covering a wide geographical or socio-economic spread; others have very focused groups to concentrate on.
- *Influence and power.* Some publics, for example active pressure groups, can gain a great deal of power, particularly if they catch the public mood. They may not be large

in number or have any direct link to the organisation, but they can be highly influential over the way an organisation conducts its business. Shell's reversal of its decision to sink the Brent Spar oil platform in the North Sea was forced by a small, but highly effective organisation (Greenpeace) galvanising public opinion. In a different way, shareholders wield a great deal of power. They have an obvious stake in an organisation and can determine its future overnight. One of the tasks of the public relations practitioner is to determine the relative influence and power of all the publics concerned, and weight the public relations programme accordingly. This is not to say that the most important publics always need to have the most money spent on them, but obviously their concerns and communication needs are paramount.

- *Connection with organisation.* Some publics are intimately connected with an organisation, for example its employees. Others have a more remote connection, for example those making an occasional visit to the Web site. Some publics will have an amicable relationship with the organisation, others will find themselves in opposition to it. Again, the public relations practitioner needs to have a clear perception of these relationships and to gauge their changing nature. Some relationships could be in danger of becoming distant or of deteriorating. Others may ameliorate over time and indeed turn from negative to positive, for example, if a pressure group's legitimate concerns are addressed. Some groups are always active, some very rarely. Furthermore, some publics may have very active sub-groups within them, whereas other sections of the same public may be apparently quiescent, but with the potential to become active. Shareholders are a classic example of this. Thus the needs not only of the whole group but parts of it also need to be considered.

SECTORAL CONSIDERATIONS

The nature of the sector in which the organisation finds itself will profoundly influence the way public relations is conducted. Public relations for a market-leading manufacturer of fast moving consumer goods is quite different from public relations for a college of further education.

Each sector has its own particular opportunities, threats and constraints. Just some of the sectors in the public or non-profit-making area are:

- education;
- government;
- National Health Service (NHS) health and medical care;
- voluntary organisations;
- charities;
- emergency services;
- the armed services;
- NGOs (non-governmental organisations), for example the World Health Organization.

Some of the organisations in these sectors are enormous and the public relations support required for a major government department such as the Department of Health or a large international charity such as Oxfam are quite as large and complex as anything that would be found in the private sector. In fact, because of the constraints placed on some of those organisations, for example the requirements of the Citizen's Charter or the need to account for every single pound spent on promotional activity, the challenges can be seen to be greater than those in private industry where it could be argued there is less direct external accountability.

The private sector, too, cannot be regarded as a uniform mass. It can be split up into the following areas:

- commerce;
- finance;
- manufacturing;
- services;
- retail.

The growing area of e-commerce can almost be regarded as a sector in its own right.

Working in the manufacturing environment where there may be great emphasis on marketing communication activities in the sales promotion area such as exhibitions, demonstrations, conferences etc can be quite different from working in commerce where the balance may be towards paper-based public relations describing various activities. Of course, multi- and new media such as I-TV (interactive television) and the Internet open up non-traditional communication, too, and offer great opportunities for public relations professionals.

There is one other sector that does not fit neatly into either public or private and that is the professions, such as accountancy, law and medicine, which straddle both.

ORGANISATIONAL DEVELOPMENT – BUSINESS STAGE

Public relations activities are often dictated by the stage of development at which an organisation finds itself.

Development depends on the sort of industry an organisation operates within. For example, in the fashion or in the hi-tech industries, development and decline can be very rapid indeed. Other industries, the motor trade or food retailing being cases in point, mature more slowly and then maintain their position. Ford Motor Company is a good example of a mature, established company.

Then there are variations within industries. The computer company Microsoft has grown very rapidly in an industry that was dominated for years by big names such as IBM.

Factors affecting organisational development are:

- the nature of the industry;
- competitor activity;
- technological impacts;
- the power of suppliers;
- the power of consumers;
- management decisions on direction;
- resources, both financial and human.

Looking at the various stages of an organisation's development reveals that there will be specific public relations requirements at different times:

- *Start-up.* Usually companies start small. The owners will know suppliers, customers and their employees, and often there will not be a separate public relations function. Public relations will be in the form of one-to-one contact with the various publics, with maybe some literature and a Web site to support the contact. The main emphasis will be on marketing communication, since growth will be a priority.
- *Growth.* With more employees and more customers, face-to-face contact may not be possible and management time will be taken up managing the business. At this stage an individual public relations practitioner or a consultancy may be employed. Public relations will still be viewed quite narrowly, largely as part of the marketing communication mix. Externally activity will focus on raising awareness of the company, its products and services. Internally there may be the beginnings of a formal communication programme including briefings, use of e-mail, notice boards, social activities and so on.

  The priority will be on expansion, and capital costs

could be quite high, especially if new premises have to be acquired. Resource constraints are likely to be a major factor influencing the role of public relations. Certainly activities like a comprehensive community relations programme are likely to be low on the agenda.

● *Maturity.* At this stage the organisation is likely to be well established. The public relations function probably will be expanded and certainly the range of activities it is involved in is likely to be considerably broadened.

It could well be that a stockmarket flotation is being considered. Capital might be needed for expansion or acquisition. If this is the case an active financial public relations campaign will be pursued.

Employee relations will be more developed. The objective will be to have an efficient and well-motivated workforce who are working to known organisational objectives and who help to maintain a competitive edge. There will also be the need to attract good-quality new staff to the organisation.

The employee relations programme will be well developed, including techniques such as employee briefings, conferences, newsletters and the full range of IT-enabled communication. Public relations may be involved in supporting the training function in producing interactive training programmes, and indeed will be using interactive media in internal and external communication programmes.

The public relations department may be assisted by one or more public relations consultancies and will be running a full corporate programme as well as continuing to support marketing efforts. The organisation should, at this stage, have a unified, cohesive identity and an established reputation. Furthermore, it should have a developed sense of corporate responsibility, as it impacts more and more on the environment in which it operates (both local and remote). It will probably be involved actively in a range of community relations projects, including sponsorships, help in kind, support of local initiatives, cause-related marketing and so on.

- **Decline.** Many companies avoid decline by adjusting their orientation or by moving into new areas of activity. However, for whatever reason, takeover, financial or legislative change, or downright bad management, some organisations move into a period of temporary or permanent decline. There is a vital role for public relations to play. Spotting the issues before they become crises is a key role (see Chapter 4 for more on this). Handling crises with honesty and integrity if they do happen (for example a major product recall, as in the case of Perrier, or a major incident such as Swiss Air's handling of the crash of flight no. SR111 in 1998, can help maintain reputation and minimise the risk of a crisis unravelling out of control.

Ultimately, if a business is non-viable, there is nothing public relations can do to rescue it. However, managing the expectations, and trying to influence the behaviour, of those publics critical to the eventual fate of an organisation in decline is very much within the remit of public relations. This is not a manipulative or unethical practice, but it is managing the situation professionally, bearing in mind the legitimate interests of all those involved.

ORGANISATIONAL CHARACTERISTICS

Knowing the organisation is imperative. There should be no skeletons unknown to the public relations practitioner, who should know the organisation inside out: history, its current status, its future plans, everything there is to know. The following headings give a framework for investigation:

- *Nature of sector.* Know the sector. What are the trends for the industry? Is it expanding, contracting and are there new, exciting markets? What is the operating environment? Is the economy in recession and are there any major issues facing the industry or the company, such as new legislation or pressing environmental demands? What is the reputation of the sector? (If the sector as a whole has a bad reputation, this is an additional problem.)

- *Competitor activity.* How is the organisation placed in relation to the competition? Is it possible to take market leadership in some or all areas? Are competitors new, aggressive young Turks likely to steal the market? Are there few or many competitors? Which ones are making headway and why? What are their weaknesses?
- *Mission.* What is the mission of the organisation? Is it to be the biggest, the best, the most innovative? Is it possible to be distinctive or will it be a 'Me too'? Is the mission realistic or a pious hope which needs to be challenged?
- *Size and structure.* How large is the organisation compared to other companies inside and outside the industry? How much 'clout' does it have? Is it a single, simple structure or a complex conglomerate? Is it hierarchical or flat, restructured or re-engineered? Does it operate in one or several countries? (Different countries have different reputations: an engineering company operating from Germany will be regarded differently from one operating from Ghana, where there is no engineering tradition.) What is the structure of the public relations operation given these factors? Is it an appropriate structure? Should consultancies be used or should everything be handled in-house?
- *Nature of the business.* What activities does the organisation perform? Is it single or multi-product? Does it operate in a single sector or several sectors? Are specialist public relations roles needed, for example is a hi-tech or construction division needed, or can all activities be served from a unified or devolved public relations department?
- *Tradition and history.* Is the company old and established or is it new with its position to establish? Is it well known for doing things in certain ways or is it an

unknown quantity? Closely linked to this is the philosophy and culture of the organisation. Is it open and participative or is it hierarchical and directive?

- *Image history.* How has the organisation been perceived over the years? Is it market-leading, innovative, reliable, plodding and slow, or slightly shifty? Has the image been constant or has it been subject to rapid or developmental change?
- *Types of employees.* White collar? Blue collar? Graduate? Semi- or unskilled? A complete mixture?

All these organisational factors profoundly affect how the public relations function is structured, and how and what the activities are that need to be carried out.

ISSUES

It is obvious that the issues affecting the society or an industry in which an organisation operates, as well as the specific issues that the organisation faces, are likely to set an agenda for much of the public relations work. Issues generally fall into a number of categories, as follows:

- *Structural.* The major long-term trends in society, such as an ageing population, technological developments, things over which the individual organisation will have very little control.
- *External.* Largely contextual issues such as environmental concerns, community concerns, political imperatives.
- *Crises.* Normally short term and arising from unforeseen events, for example a factory disaster, war, product recall.
- *Internal.* Long- or short-term issues that are facing the company from within, for example succession policy and industrial relations.

- *Current affairs.* Those things that are of immediate public interest and which often are the subject of intense media coverage at the time, for example, dangerous dogs legislation following a series of dog attacks reported in the media, gun legislation.
- *Potential.* Those issues that have not yet emerged. It might seem rather odd to list this, but it is very much the case that some issues do appear to arise from nowhere, except that the careful practitioner will have an intelligence system at his or her disposal that can give early warning of potential issues likely to become real. Content analysis of the media can often give an indicator of what may be on the public agenda in the future, and is a vastly underutilised resource by organisations. Also, contact with think tanks, the scientific community and futures groups can provide a rich picture of possible scenarios.

PUBLIC OPINION

Public opinion, often expressed through the media, or even encouraged by the media, is a very potent influence on organisations. The campaign against genetically modified organisms in the United Kingdom led to the withdrawal of genetically modified foods from many supermarkets. Those at the forefront of research in this area, for example Monsanto, had to modify their plans for development as a result and government-approved trials were disrupted.

The media as a reflector of public opinion is vital to public relations because the same channel is often used to put across public relations messages. The media often define and crystalise the public mood, although sometimes its influence can be overestimated.

It is certainly true that the media can fatally damage the reputation of an organisation or individual. Sometimes this is because the organisation is genuinely at fault, in which case the media is doing its job of serving the public interest.

Sometimes, as libel cases attest, there is little ground for their attacks.

It is also the case that the media can massively enhance the reputation of an organisation by offering free publicity for the good work that it is doing or by favourably reporting on its business performance. This is especially true if comment is made in influential media such as the *Financial Times* if a financial matter is being reported, or in the tabloids and relevant consumer press if a consumer product is being promoted.

TIMESCALES

Obviously timescales are critical when determining public relations programmes. Sometimes the practitioner has the luxury of planning a programme over a self-selected period of time. The reality often is, however, that either external or internal restraints, or both, determine when activities can be performed.

- *Externally driven timescales.* Quite frequently external factors determine when public relations activities take place. If, for example, an organisation wants to change a clause in some proposed legislation, it has to undertake its lobbying within the time frame laid down by Parliament. Other factors such as the announcement of financial results are regulated by the Stock Exchange rules. Information regarding competitive activity may lead to pre-emptive action within very precise time limits.
- *Internally driven timescales.* Examples of internally imposed deadlines are the introduction of a new product, the arrival of a new chief executive, a decision to build a new production line, achievement of an international quality standard and so on.

RESOURCES

The level of resources put into a public relations function or department clearly determines the level and scope of activities that can be undertaken. The resourcing of specific programmes is discussed in Chapter 8. However, it is appropraite here to cover it briefly.

Normally there are two approaches. The first is to determine an appropriate departmental structure along with the relevant activities that need to be undertaken, and to provide the human and financial resources to implement them.

The second approach is to devote a budget to public relations, broadly in line with the resourcing also given to other departments in the organisation. For example, 10 per cent of the overall marketing budget is a figure sometimes quoted. The trick then is to prioritise the public relations activities and to carry out those essential elements of the programme within budget.

What is absolutely guaranteed is that the ideal budget will always be considerably more than that allocated! But that's life and public relations practitioners like everyone else have to live within their budgets.

While the other six areas give an overall context to public relations, it is true to say that timescales and resources are constraining factors on activity.

3

Starting the planning process

GETTING IN CONTROL

Having looked at public relations within the business context and recognising the ways in which public relations can be structured and conducted, we can now look at the planning process itself.

Public relations practitioners are very busy individuals. First of all they have operational responsibilities like anyone else who works in a disciplined environment. If they hold a management role they have to handle budgets and people, run an effective department or consultancy, control suppliers, ensure quality standards are met and so on. In fact, all the skills required of any manager are required of public relations professionals.

There are also other pressures. Much of the work is high profile. A mistake made when talking to a journalist has very public consequences. In fact, most of the activities of public relations professionals is by definition 'public'. It's a profession where there are very few ground rules: the practice is not highly prescribed as it is for other professions, such as accountancy and law. Often the role is not properly understood by colleagues. The work is usually undertaken under deadline and there is always too much to do. There are severe qualitative and quantitative pressures on practitioners.

The public relations brief is a large one: to manage the communication interface between the organisation and all its publics. That is a very tall order.

To succeed, a systematic, efficient approach to the job in hand is essential. As far as possible you need to be in control, although total control in the dynamic world of communication is impossible and not even desirable.

WHY PLANNING IS IMPORTANT

It is quite legitimate to ask 'Why plan'? There is always so much to do, why not just get on and do it?

Apart from the vital fact of putting you in control, as discussed in Chapter 1, there are several other good reasons for planning:

- *It focuses effort.* It ensures the unnecessary is excluded. It makes you work on the right things. It helps you to work smart instead of just working hard. It enables you to operate efficiently and effectively because you are concentrating on the priorities.
- *It improves effectiveness.* By working on the right things, defined objectives will be achieved. Time and money will be saved because effort isn't being diverted into worthy but less important tasks. Importantly it makes saying 'No' to unplanned things much easier. Or at

least you can say, 'If I take on this task, which of my other prioritised jobs should I drop?' In other words working to planned objectives gives you targets to aim for, a sense of achievement when they are reached, and effective benchmarks for measurement.

● *It encourages the long-term view.* By definition, to plan you have to look ahead. This forces you to take a longer perspective than the immediate here and now. It forces you to look back and evaluate past achievements, to look around at the organisation and its priorities and at the broader business context, and it helps you to produce a structured programme to meet future as well as current needs.

● *It helps demonstrate value for money.* This is applicable whether working in-house or in consultancy. If there is a fight for budgets, then demonstrating past achievements and being able to present a powerful, costed, forward-looking and realistic programme gives you a point from which to argue your case for money.

● *It minimises mishaps.* Careful planning means that at the macro level different scenarios have been considered and the most appropriate selected. It means that there is meticulous contingency planning and all the angles have been covered. At the micro level, planning makes day-to-day work tolerable, even fun.

● *It reconciles conflicts.* When putting together a programme or a campaign there are always conflicts of interests and priorities. Planning helps you confront those difficulties before they arise and to work them through to resolution. Sometimes this can mean difficult discussions with and decisions about other colleagues in different departments, but better to sort that out at the planning stage than in the middle of a complex, time-constrained programme.

● *It facilitates proactivity.* Setting your own agenda is vitally important. Of course public relations work is about reacting to media demands or responding quickly to a crisis, but it is also about deciding what you want to do – what actions you want to take, what messages you want to put across and when. Planning a comprehensive and cohesive programme helps you achieve this.

Planning applies to everything, whether it is to complete programmes and campaigns lasting one or five years or even longer, or to individual activities such as a press conference or the briefing of suppliers.

PUBLIC RELATIONS POLICY

The first requirement is for a clear public relations policy to be laid down. This should define the remit of public relations activity and set the ground rules for operation.

The idea of a policy is not to be regulatory and restrictive, but to give the rules of engagement so that everyone knows where responsibility lies, where the lines of demarcation are and, ultimately, who is accountable for what activities.

Policy statements need not be long or complicated, but they must be clear.

Figure 3.1 shows an example from Pilkington PLC of its corporate public relations policy. Pilkington has a group (corporate) public relations function which deals largely with company-wide matters and which agreed this policy with senior management. It also has several divisions and subsidiaries that have their own public relations activities.

CORPORATE PUBLIC RELATIONS POLICY

1. Meetings with the City press must be kept at a level consistent with maintaining satisfactory relationships and will be arranged through Group Public Relations.

    Statements to the City press may be made only by

General Board directors, or by Group Public Relations acting on the Board's instructions.

2. The Group will not normally publicise through the media its attitudes to matters that are politically sensitive at local or national level. Considerable time is expended by directors and some senior managers on representing the company's interests to legislators, parliamentarians, and others with the ability to affect the company's future; these contacts can be prejudiced by inopportune publicity.

3. The Group will not offer public comment on the wisdom or otherwise of budgetary or other legislative measures. It may be prepared to give factual evidence about the effects of such measures on the performance of any part of the Group when such effects can be demonstrated.

4. Public comment, in the press or elsewhere, must relate to historic or current activities. Comment about future plans and/or prospects must be avoided so far as is practicable.

5. Announcements about possible or planned capital investments or disinvestments may not normally be made until such projects have been formally authorised by the General Board.

    Where local or national government agencies need to be consulted in advance of an investment, it may be necessary to make an earlier announcement. In such cases, the limited extent of the commitment at that stage must be emphasised. Dates for starting or completing projects must be given in a form that will allow for contingencies.

6. No announcements should be made about negotiations, eg licensing agreements, co-operative agreements with other companies, until negotiations are successfully completed and the form of announcement has been agreed by the parties concerned.

7. Opportunities for favourable publicity will be identified by Group Public Relations and exploited after clearance at Executive Director level.

8. Divisions, subsidiaries and functions retaining external public relations advisers in whatever capacity should ensure that the constraints of their role are very clearly defined, if necessary in consultation with Group Public Relations.

   Under no circumstances must retained advisers be permitted to make public statements on behalf of Pilkington, or to lobby on behalf of Pilkington, without prior clearance through Group Public Relations.
9. Where circumstances suggest that action should be taken which would be at variance with these guidelines, such action should not be taken without prior clearance from the Chairman or a Deputy Chairman, with the involvement of Group Public Relations.
10. Divisions, subsidiaries and functions should ensure that Group Public Relations are briefed and consulted on all occasions where these guidelines have a relevance.

    These guidelines are not intended to restrict divisional public relations activities in the marketing area where there is established liaison with Group Public Relations.

Figure 3.1 *Pilkington PLC corporate public relations policy*

Once the areas of operation have been confirmed, activities can be planned and managed.

BASIC QUESTIONS IN PLANNING

The planning process is really quite simple. The trick is to break things down into a manageable sequence. It is helpful to ask five basic questions:

What do I want to achieve? (What are my objectives?)
Who do I want to talk to? (Who are my publics?)
What do I want to say? (What are the messages I want to get across?)

How shall I say it?	(What mechanisms shall I use to get my messages across?)
How do I know I've got it right?	(How will I evaluate my work?)

And the purpose of the activity is to influence behaviour in some way, not forgetting that this includes the possibility of the organisation changing as well as its publics.

In order to answer these questions there are two major requirements:

● *Information.* Finding out everything there is to know about the task in hand – careful research and analysis.
● *Strategy.* Using that information to identify the guiding principles and main thrust of the programme.

From these two requirements comes the tactical programme that can be evaluated for effectiveness.

At this stage it should be noted that the list of questions includes questions about information-seeking and research (objectives, publics, messages and evaluation), but only one question about the actual doing.

This is about the right proportion of effort that should go into the planning process. Get the research and analysis right, and the programme should then virtually write itself. Please note, it is not being suggested that 80 per cent of the time spent on a programme overall should be put into information-seeking. That is plainly wrong as you would never get anything done. However, 80 per cent of the effort put into devising an appropriate programme should go into research. Once having put all that work into planning, the implementation should run smoothly and effectively.

All planning models follow a basic pattern, whether they are for the strategic management of an organisation or for a public relations programme. There are four basic steps as shown in Figure 3.2.

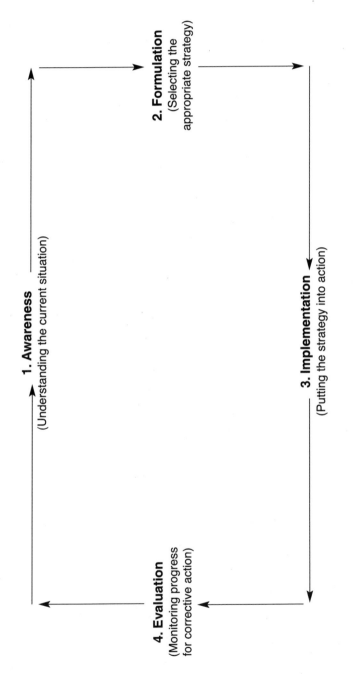

1. Awareness
(Understanding the current situation)

2. Formulation
(Selecting the
appropriate strategy)

3. Implementation
(Putting the strategy into action)

4. Evaluation
(Monitoring progress
for corrective action)

Figure 3.2   *The strategic management process*

American academics Scott Cutlip, Allen Center and Glen Broom[1] visualise the planning and management of public relations programmes as shown in Figure 3.3.

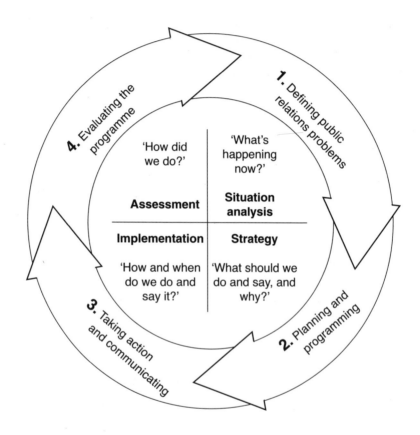

Figure 3.3 *Cutlip, Center and Broom's planning and management model*

[1]Cutlip, S M, Center, A H and Broom, G N (2000) *Effective Public Relations*, Prentice-Hall International, Upper Saddle River, New Jersey8th edn.

THE 10 STAGES OF PLANNING

To expand on the above, we can look at a sequence of planning steps that will ensure an effective programme (long-term, multi-activity programme with long-term objectives, eg a five-year corporate relations programme) or campaign (individual campaign with very specific short-term objectives, eg a media campaign to launch a new product) is put together:

- analysis;
- objectives;
- publics (audiences);
- messages;
- strategy;
- tactics;
- timescales;
- resources;
- evaluation;
- review.

Sometimes the analysis and objectives are in reverse order. An organisation might give its public relations department or consultancy a list of objectives it wants them to achieve. However, these objectives must be carefully scrutinised in order to see if they are appropriate. For example, the organisation may say it has a problem recruiting good new staff, in which case the public relations objective would be to help attract new recruits from the community. After careful analysis, the public relations professionals may discover that the real problem is not recruitment, but retention of good staff, thus the objectives of the programme will have to change and an internal rather than external campaign will have to be mounted which addresses employment policies as well as communication issues.

The planning process is illustrated in Figure 3.4.

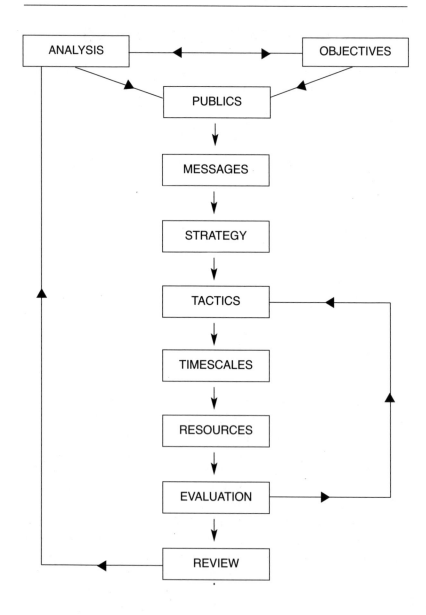

Figure 3.4   *The planning process in logical steps*

The planning process looks quite straightforward when laid out like this. However, there are often problems in practice. Sometimes there is a lack of detailed information on which to base the plan. This may be because senior managers are not prepared to share the wider game-plan, or it may be that a client only wants to give a consultancy limited information for reasons of confidentiality. Perhaps the campaign itself is very complex or fast moving, for example a complicated takeover bid. It could be that the plan is being executed under extreme time pressure, in a crisis even. It is often the case that the resources devoted to programmes are less than ideal and so corners have to be cut or the programme pruned. There also is the possibility that there are conflicting priorities arising part-way through the programme that require energy and resources to be diverted from the original course of action.

The planning scheme outlined does give a solid basis for planning and the pattern can be followed whatever the scale of the task. If the programme is particularly large it may be necessary to split it down into a series of projects that follow the same steps. Thus you might have a public affairs programme and a community relations programme, each with focused objectives and restricted publics, which feed into an overall programme with wider objectives and broader publics and messages. This is illustrated in Figure 3.5 on page 46.

There are two things that should be noted here. First, objectives need to be tied into organisational objectives (see Chapter 5). Second, as described here, the planning process could be perceived to be mechanistic and inflexible. This is not the case. The process described gives a framework for planning. In reality, time and events move on, sometimes very quickly, and public relations practitioners must be prepared to respond to changing circumstances. All the best-laid plans must be capable of being flexed or developed, and indeed scrapped altogether if necessary. These possibilities should be taken into account and welcomed. It is not a crime to move beyond what is planned if that is sensible and appropriate! However, having a framework does provide structure and coherence. The absence of a plan can indicate the lack of a strategic approach and sometimes a lack of capability. Having a plan indicates professionalism and accountability. It is plain good management and not only assures the organisation that public relations will make a valuable and agreed contribution, but provides security and a level of stability for the practitioner.

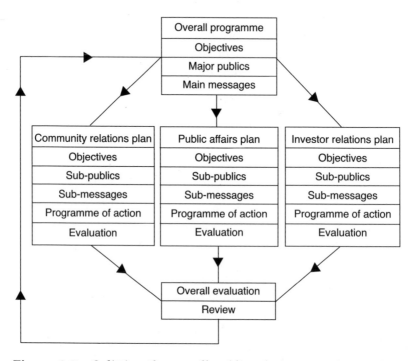

Figure 3.5 *Splitting the overall public relations programme into manageable sub-sections*

Of course it goes without saying that planning is an aid to effective working and not an end in itself. It is not meant to be a straitjacket. We live in a complex and changing environment where flexibility and adaptability are essential. We all know the kind of person who says that because something has not been planned it cannot be done. In public relations, of all disciplines, there has to be a capability to react and adjust to the dynamic organisational and communications environment in which we operate. Sometimes objectives and tactics have to change – rapidly. That's life in public relations.

Plans are made to ensure that we focus on what's necessary and achieve what we are meant to. Once laid down, they are not in tablets of stone – realism is everything. However, the planning process holds good, even if programmes have to be adjusted, and the steps given in Figure 3.2 are valid whatever changes are needed.

4

Analysis

THE FIRST PLANNING STEP

Analysis is the first part of the planning process. This entails research in order to identify the issues on which to base your public relations programme. Without getting to the core issues you will not have a credible or effective programme, or one that addresses corporate objectives.

If the core issue is that your organisation and products are regarded as old-fashioned and therefore you are losing credibility and market share, your programme will have to be about demonstrating that your organisation is forward looking and your products are modern and leading edge (provided that they are), not that you are cheaper than your competitors!

There isn't room in this book to look at the whole area of research in public relations. Complete volumes have been written on the subject. However, it is possible to give an overview.

When starting a department or a full programme from scratch (for example, following a large merger), the contextual research outlined in Chapter 2 is vital. However, if the public relations function is established and the planned programme or campaign is a continuation of an ongoing activity, then it probably is not necessary. Nevertheless, it is important and illuminating to conduct this contextual research from time to time and some of it (for example, media content monitoring) should be ongoing anyway.

For new campaigns or programmes it is vitally important to look afresh at not only the micro environment and the immediate things that affect the organisation, but also the macro environment. The macro environment is external to the organisation and it is important to know about the external forces that are impacting on both the organisation itself and its internal and external publics. The pressures, issues and imperatives that provide the context for the attitudes and decisions of publics need to be known by the public relations practitioner so that he or she can frame a programme with these matters taken into account.

PEST ANALYSIS

A commonly used and immensely valuable technique for analysing the external environment is a PEST analysis. PEST divides the overall environment into four areas and covers just about everything that can affect an organisation. The four areas are: Political, Economic, Social and Technological.

The main questions to ask when undertaking a PEST analysis are:

- What are the environmental factors that affect the organisation?
- Which of these are currently most important?
- Which will be most important in the next four years?

The grid below gives some headings that could be considered under the four areas.

POLITICAL	ECONOMIC
Environmental legislation	Interest rates
Employment legislation	Inflation
Trade (including overseas)	Money supply
legislation	Levels of employment
Change/continuance of	Disposable income
government	Business/economic cycles
	World business/economic
	conditions
	Energy costs
SOCIAL	**TECHNOLOGICAL**
Population shifts and growth	New discoveries
Lifestyles	Rate of change
Levels of education	Investment in technology
Income/wealth distribution	Spending on research and
Consumer purchasing trends	development
Social attitudes and concerns	Obsolescence
	Impact of new technologies

Some experts recommend an expanded version of PEST, believing the original no longer does justice to the complex environment in which modern organisations operate. A popular acronym is EPISTLE. Here, as well as the four elements of PEST, separate consideration is given to Information, the Legal (or regulatory) aspects and the physical (or Green) Environment. Information, as they say, is power. Thus the access to and availability of information is critical to organisations. The ubiquity and power of the Internet makes this element of the environment even more potent.

The legal environment in which organisations operate is increasingly complex and apart from national considerations there are transnational regulations such as EU law and international agreements such as GATT. Furthermore, there are quasi-legal restraints, including the 'moral' undertakings that governments make, such as the commitment to reduce pollution, in which organisations have a part to play.

The physical environment in which we live is judged to be one of *the* major concerns of the 21st century. The impact of global warming, pressures to radically alter transport systems, sustainability, waste disposal, etc, are all 'hot' topics and organisations will need to be aware of the drivers for change and the issues facing them as a result.

In addition, some analysts recommend that 'culture' merits specific consideration. Organisations need to recognise and take into account the diverse religious and social cultures prevalent in the different countries in which they operate or trade. Also, sensitivity is required to organisational culture and the different norms and values that exist between organisations that work even within the same sector. IBM is very different from Microsoft.

Of course, it doesn't really matter which acronym you use for your analysis as long as all the elements are covered. The point of doing such analyses is to identify the main drivers that will impact on the organisation. These drivers will be different, depending on the country, industry and organisation being analysed – there are no stock responses.

It is also important to establish the interrelationships between these drivers. World economic trends may affect political decisions and technological developments may affect social aspects of life. For example, the technological developments in games technology has transformed the lives of many young people, especially boys. In turn, their adroitness at using the technology has spurred on further technological advances.

Having generated a list of possible external environmental influences, the main ones have to be identified, and it is imperative to be as specific as possible to the organisation under consideration. So, for example, someone working in the higher education field in the Western world will have to consider the following three drivers among others. The first is to do with demographics; the proportion of people under 21 is decreasing so the higher education system will have to adapt itself to teaching a higher proportion of mature students. The second is that the use of technology in teaching is transforming the traditional teacher/student relationship. Third, the requirement for a higher proportion of the population to have at least first degree level qualifications or their equivalent means there will be more students in the higher education system demanding resources, yet those resources are critically dependent on the economic state of individual countries and the priorities that governments put on education.

PEST analysis also helps to identify the long-term drivers of change. For example, some markets are becoming more global and it is vital to identify the factors involved in that, such as the use of technology. The worldwide similarity of consumer tastes in some areas such as soft drinks, electronic goods and sport leads to opportunities for global approaches to marketing and manufacturing.

The PEST analysis process can also identify how external influences can affect organisations in different ways. So a company that traditionally sources its raw materials from a number of countries is less likely to be vulnerable to a political crisis than a company that sources its raw materials from a single, cheaper supplier in a country with a less stable political regime. In fact, the move to globalisation has been partly driven by companies being alert to the threats inherent in single-source suppliers, single-location markets and their own vulnerability to exchange-rate fluctuations.

Some organisations are more affected by one of the four PEST areas than others. For example, the political context is vitally important to local government, whereas economic factors may be more important to retailing organisations.

It is interesting to note how this kind of analysis matches classic strategic business planning as demonstrated in Figure 4.1.

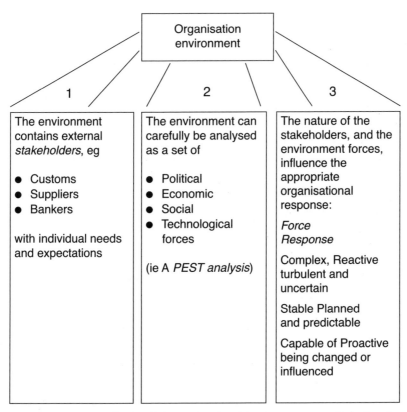

Figure 4.1 *Analysis of Organisation Environment undertaken in strategic planning*[1]

The difference is that for public relations the focus will be on communication issues.

SPOTTING THE ISSUES

PEST analyses are done at particular points in time – something that is sometimes forgotten. They should be undertaken for the current situation and for different situations that

---

[1]Thompson, J L (1995) *Strategy in Action*, Chapman & Hall, London

might occur in the future. So in scenario planning, the most likely key drivers are given different weightings and alternative futures are envisaged, together with associated plans of action.

By carrying out a thorough-going PEST analysis, which looks not only at current but also future developments, it is possible to identify the potentially most significant issues that might affect the organisation and to track those issues. A number of the media monitoring companies now offer an issues analysis service. They not only track what are the most prevalent issues of the day overall (for example, views on current economic performance), but also spot those issues that are emerging on to the agenda because they are beginning to attract media coverage.

Forward-looking companies spend a great deal of time and effort on issues management. They constantly scan the wider environment to determine which issues they should be paying particular regard to. Issues that are not identified or not taken seriously have a nasty habit of coming back to haunt you as crises.

Issues management works in two ways:

● It identifies those issues over which the organisation can have no control, where public opinion is inevitably going to move in a particular direction and therefore it would be foolish for the company to maintain or take up a position that flies in the face of the prevailing view. It would be very odd if an organisation in the West were to promulgate the view that large families are to be encouraged when a major concern is overpopulation.

In this situation an organisation has to examine its policies and practices, and bring them into line with public opinion, or it risks losing the sympathy and support of its stakeholders.

Organisations that are adept at issues management not only handle current issues, but also predict the likely public reaction to emerging concerns and position themselves as leaders by changing their policies and practices or adopting new ones ahead of anyone else. They can be seen to be leading the field rather than being forced to react because of prevailing opinion. They do this not just to get ahead, but because they are progressive, ethical and responsive to the likely demands of their stakeholders.

● It detects those issues where the organisation can have an input into the emerging debate and therefore shape its outcome in an ethical and beneficial way. An example of this is Rhone-Poulenc Agriculture's 10-year experiment looking at organic versus conventional farming (ie farming with agro-chemicals), which is trying to determine the best farming method, economically, environmentally and in food quality terms. By establishing the facts about both systems, the company will be able to make a definitive contribution to the debate. It will also be bound by the results, whatever they are.

Thus issues analysis works in both directions: detecting those external factors, political, economic, social or technological that require the company to change; and identifying those areas where it might have an input into the public debate and influence the outcome.

Any comprehensive public relations programme must address long-term issues. Individual public relations campaigns must also identify any relevant issues which, depending on the nature of the campaign, may be long or short term. Obviously a campaign to launch an individual car care product will not require such a wide-ranging examination of the issues as a five-year programme to relaunch and reposition a charity.

In summary, it is important to know the broad organisational context, the organisation itself, the issues affecting the organisation, the mood of public opinion, and the views and aspirations of stakeholders (groups of individuals who can influence the performance of an organisation, for example employees, customers and suppliers – more on this in Chapter 6).

Having analysed the broader environmental context it is necessary to apply these specifically to the organisation.

SWOT ANALYSIS

One way to approach this is to divide these considerations by SWOT analysis. The first two elements, Strengths and Weaknesses, can be seen as internally driven and particular to the organisation. The other two, Opportunities and Threats, are normally external and will have been largely identified through the PEST analysis. The four elements can be seen as mirror segments in a quadrant. Below is a brief example.

STRENGTHS	WEAKNESSES
Financially strong	Conservative in investment
Innovative	Restricted product line
Good leadership	Traditional and hierarchical
Good reputation	Complacent
Loyal workforce	Inflexible working patterns
OPPORTUNITIES	THREATS
Cheap supplies from Eastern Europe	Instability of Eastern Bloc
To expand into China	Danger of being overstretched
To acquire competitors	To be taken over by conglomerate

It is sometimes useful to apply SWOT analysis to categories of activity, for example corporate, product, internal and so on. This wide-ranging research of the external and internal environment, which also includes the contextual research outlined in Chapter 2, was called 'environmental monitoring' (or scanning) by Otto Lerbinger, who in his seminal work[1] described the various types of public relations research.

A legitimate question might be why should the public relations person be involved in all this research, after all our business is communication? It is precisely because the business is communication that practitioners need to be alert to the drivers affecting an organisation – probably as much if not more than anyone else in the organisation. The purpose of communication is to help an organisation meet its objectives. If a public relations professional is not aware of the drivers that frame company objectives, how can he or she fulfil the boundary-spanning communication role described earlier (see Chapter 1)?

Taking the above analysis into consideration we can see that our public relations programme will have a number of jobs to do in support of corporate objectives. For example, we will need to mount a marketing communications campaign if our product line is to be expanded. We will want an internal communications programme to assist in managing change. An international corporate and government relations campaign will be required if we are to expand into China, and we will certainly need a financial relations programme if we are to preserve our strong reputation, raise capital to fund expansion and offset takeover possibilities.

WHAT STATE THE STAKEHOLDER?

Having determined from an organisational point of view what the key issues are and the organisation's stance on them,

[1]Lerbinger, O (1972) *Designs for Persuasive Communication*, Prentice-Hall, Englewood Cliffs, NJ.

it is then the public relations professional's job to create a public relations programme with objectives that address those issues.

Before doing that, however, the state of the relationship between the organisation and its stakeholders also needs analysis. If the view that stakeholders have of an organisation differs from the actual facts of the case, there is a further issue that needs to be addressed. Lerbinger calls the type of research that defines publics and finds out how they perceive an organisation before, during and after a campaign 'public relations audits'. The problem may be lack of information, or wrong information, that can be countered quite easily. The problem might be more profound or complex, for example, the organisation might have a reputation for being a bad employer because it had to make 50 per cent of its workforce redundant to survive several years before and the legacy lingers on.

You then have to discover if a real communication problem exists, what the actual problem is, with whom (which stakeholders), what messages need to be communicated, how they should be communicated and whether or not they are effective. Lerbinger calls the kind of research that evaluates whether or not messages have got through to the targeted audiences 'communications audits'. 'Social audits' research the consequences of an organisation's actions on its publics and monitor corrective actions; this kind of research may need to be done before a campaign starts, particularly if the campaign is as a result of the organisation's action, as is often the case in crises.

So research is required or, more accurately, 'intelligence' – ie assimilated and interpreted information. It is impossible to change thoughts, attitudes or behaviour without knowing what the starting point is.

It is worth saying that research shouldn't just be done when a programme is being planned. It should be an ongoing process. It should be used to monitor the progress of a programme or campaign and it should certainly be used to evaluate effectiveness once a campaign has ended (more on this in Chapter 9).

The number of times a complete review of an organisation and its communication takes place is quite rare. It usually happens when the public relations function is just established, when a new head is appointed or if there is a strategic review. Consultancies, when pitching for business, will, as part of their background research, undertake this kind of analysis to a greater or lesser extent.

However, most practitioners are involved in planning full programmes or short campaigns and the same basic disciplines apply. Research around the topic in hand needs to be rigorous and objective, but it need not necessarily be expensive – it depends on the task. If you want to find out the views of the local community, it is a simple matter to walk the streets and ask, to go to the local pubs, to ask the local Rotary or Lions clubs and to speak to local community leaders. This might be all that is needed. If, however, you want to launch a major campaign aimed at changing the country's eating habits, much more detailed and sophisticated research will be required.

The principles behind doing research are the same whether they are for major, strategic, long-term programmes or short campaigns. Research helps you establish what the nature and style of the communication task is, what the objectives should be, what publics should be addressed, what messages and methods should be employed, and whether or not you have succeeded in your objectives.

Sometimes the communication task seems obvious, but research doesn't just tell you what you need to communicate. A company may want to fight proposed legislation that threatens a large part of its business. Research will reveal the size of the task, the best way to tackle it (messages and mechanisms) and also indicate the chances of success – there is no point in spending money on lost causes.

WHO SHOULD UNDERTAKE THE RESEARCH?

Given that whole programmes or campaigns are based on research, it is important that it is carried out properly. It is not good enough to instruct the most junior member of the public relations team to contact a few customers to find out what they think of the existing corporate identity. Those involved in serious research must be properly trained. There is no point in spending money getting biased or incomplete answers. There are several excellent short courses and textbooks on conducting research. You don't have to spend a fortune to become competent at collecting basic information and interpreting it properly.

Obviously, if you employ an established research consultancy or use trained in-house people, they will know all about undertaking statistically valid research, which involves selecting a sample that genuinely reflects the universe being studied.

Sometimes it is entirely legitimate to do a 'quick and dirty' study of, for example, reactions of personal finance journalists to a new pension plan, as long as you recognise the limitations of that study and don't try to use it as anything other than a fairly superficial survey of a very particular group of people.

The benefits of using trained in-house researchers are that they know the business and will need little briefing except for the specifics of the research problem. On the downside, they may be seen to be less objective than external researchers and there is always the syndrome of the prophet honoured everywhere but in his own country to contend with.

External researchers could very well offer specialist skills in specialised research areas, including communication. They may be perceived to be more objective, but are often (although not necessarily) more expensive because they build in learning time, overheads, profits and so on.

Of course, it is perfectly possible to mix the two. You could get professional advice on questionnaire design, administer it yourself and get a research company to analyse the results for you.

RESEARCH TECHNIQUES

There are several different types of research. First of all there is quantitative research which collects data that is then, expressed statistically giving results in numbers or quantities, and there is qualitative research, which investigates non-quantifiable variables such as opinions, reactions and attitudes. Thus, measuring how many people will vote for a particular party at a general election is quantitative research; finding out what views an individual has on the policies of the major political parties is qualitative research.

Continuous or tracking research is where the same group of people or people of the same profile are asked the same questions at regular intervals. Television companies often have a panel of viewers whom they will contact regularly to find out what they have viewed and what their opinions are of various programmes. Building societies regularly survey groups of people on a one-off basis, but with the same characteristics, to find out what awareness of the various societies is. The large research companies frequently survey business people to discover all kinds of things, from their views on the economy to opinions on executive pay.

Surveys have been undertaken on just about anything from how many people with blue eyes like baked beans to what people thought of France's performance in the last football World Cup.

Continuous or tracking surveys are particularly helpful when trying to measure something like consumer trends or changes in attitude over time. One-off surveys are useful if you need some definitive factual information on which to base a campaign. For example, you will want to know what proportion of the population buys wigs before you launch a new kind of wig.

Then there is primary and secondary research. Secondary research is often called desk research and entails collecting information from already published sources. There is an enormous amount of published data that can be accessed. The trick is knowing where to find it. Public and university libraries have vast collections of material on companies and industry sectors, social trends and so on. They are often connected to international information databases. They also have newspapers and magazines archived on databases and CD ROM, as do trade libraries run by professional bodies such as the Law Society. Government departments hold statistics on subjects relevant to them. Company reports and corporate and product literature are available from most organisations. Almost everything under the sun has been surveyed at some stage and most libraries are happy to point you in the right direction if you ask nicely. The Internet also provides huge possibilities for obtaining information from individuals and organisations worldwide. Much of the information available in libraries is now also available on the Internet and there are several research companies that are capitalising on the almost insatiable appetite for information. Many journalists, especially the specialists, use the Internet as their primary information source and it is a rich if sometimes frustrating mine of information. It also has the advantage of being up to date (usually!).

The large research companies such as Mintel, MORI and Gallup conduct their own surveys on various topics, and you can ask for a listing and buy their reports very easily, either as hard copy or electronically. Of course desk research takes time and hiring the services of a professional researcher could make the task much easier if time means money to you. However, research that has already been conducted is often a great deal cheaper than doing the work yourself. A quick call or an e-mail and a small fee to a research organisation to find out what's available could save you a great deal of money.

Primary research is finding out the information you want at first hand. There are various techniques for obtaining primary data.

Self-completion questionnaires

These are a relatively cheap way to contact a large number of people over a geographically widespread area (or even a small number of people in a geographically tight area). They are excellent for obtaining information from people who are difficult to contact (maybe they are shift workers) and they allow time for people to consider their answers carefully before responding. It is useful to include an incentive (for example, free entry to a prize draw) to encourage a good response. Self-completion questionnaires need to be clear, simple and as short as possible. They can be distributed and collected by post, in person or via another medium such as a magazine, and are usually completed by the respondent without supervision. If a questionnaire is more complex it can be issued to groups, with a trained researcher supervising the session or answering questions that may arise.

Questionnaires are often used to obtain a mass of quantitative data, but can also be used for qualitative material. Good questionnaires that are unbiased, unambiguous and which collect all the information that is required are very difficult to design. Professional help must often be sought from trained researchers.

One-to-one interviews

This survey technique is excellent for collecting qualitative data. Interviews are obviously time consuming for the researcher and the interviewee, and this method is very expensive if a mass of data is required. There are ways in which you can keep the cost of interviewing down. It is relatively cheap to participate in an omnibus survey which may be run by one of the larger research organisations. They often undertake regular surveys on specific groups such as teenagers and industry sectors like motoring, and on particular products such as computer games. You can add a few questions to the survey and you are charged per question. Results from these interviews can usually be turned around very quickly, often with a few days.

There are also syndicated studies where the results are available to those who subscribe to the service. The survey mentioned earlier where building societies track awareness is a syndicated study with the participating building societies obtaining the results for a fee.

Although relatively expensive, the quality and quantity of information that can be gathered from tailor-made one-to-one interviews can be superb. Again it is important to stress that interviewing is a particular skill and training is required to get the best from the opportunity. Interviews can be structured so that specific information is collected, unstructured where the questions are developed as a result of the answers given, or somewhere in between – semi-structured.

Interviewing allows the researcher to explore views and opinions in depth, and the reasons why those views are held. When trying to get to the heart of difficult issues it is an excellent technique to use. Sophisticated computer programs are now available to analyse text, picking out key words and phrases, and facilitate quantitative as well as qualitative analysis.

Telephone interviews

This technique is particularly suitable for collecting structured information. They are a kind of halfway house between face-to-face interviews and questionnaires. They don't allow as much probing as the face-to-face interview or the reflection of the questionnaire, but they are a relatively speedy way to collect information from a broad or narrow section of respondents. The Computer Aided Telephone Interview (CATI) system allows researchers to input answers to questions very quickly and instant analysis is possible. CATI systems also provide call management facilities such as organising calls, redialling engaged numbers and keeping statistics of failed contacts.

Focus groups

Focus groups are discussion groups comprising carefully selected individuals (maybe with the same profile, for example 20- to 25-year-old Asian women, married with children, all born in the UK and living in Cardiff; or maybe of the same age, gender and location, but with very different backgrounds). Running a successful focus group is a highly skilled activity and requires a competent co-ordinator to guide discussion and to ensure all the relevant questions are asked. The idea behind a focus group is that the responses from the participants prompt and develop responses from other participants. Properly done, focus groups can obtain far more information than one-to-one interviews. There are difficulties associated with this technique: selection of participants, length of time needed, facilities required (room, recording equipment), expense (travel costs, refreshments), but the depth of insight that can be acquired is a rich reward.

Internet groups

As well as gathering information from various sources on the Internet, it is very easy to undertake one-to-one or group research. Visitors to your Web site can be asked to fill in a short questionnaire or to make comments on particular subjects. You can set up a bulletin board or host a chat room on your site.

The use of e-mail, intranets and extranets means that contacting and obtaining the views of specific groups of people, for example employees or suppliers, is simple and fast. Of course, the temptation to go back to these sources repeatedly (to the point of annoyance), because it is so easy, must be resisted. On the other hand, the opportunity to set up a genuine and ongoing dialogue with stakeholders in which research is an integral part is something that it would be irresponsible to miss.

Informal research

Apart from the formal research techniques, there are all kinds of ways of obtaining information about issues and organisations. Chance encounters and informal discussions with the whole range of publics associated with an organisation such as competitors, specialist journalists, neighbours and suppliers can be very enlightening. Getting a feel for the organisation by attending its annual general meeting or social events helps. Don't just talk to the self-important people: cleaners, secretaries and security people are important too, and are often more honest and realistic. Regular reading of the quality press, listening to and watching general interest and current affairs programmes, even discussions with friends and colleagues in social situations, help to build an all-embracing overview of the context and the specifics of any particular situation, and help you make connections between these issues and organisations that might not be available via formal research.

Informal, or 'quick and dirty' research, should not be discounted either. A very successful campaign to save a London hospital was based on the public relations executive walking the streets surrounding the hospital asking people about it and talking to people in the pub. Oh, and the executive had a lot of experience in public relations! Not a procedure recommended as exemplary, but time was pressing and it worked!

Media research

It is important not only to know your organisation and the relevant issues, but to investigate the channels of communication too. The written and broadcast media provide information on readership profiles, circulation, effectiveness of advertising, reaction to copy and so on. Other media such as direct mail, advertising, posters and sponsorship can also be analysed. The various media have their own trade bodies that can provide all kinds of information on their use and effectiveness, and this should be carefully considered when deciding which channels should be used for particular publics.

Communication audit

Apart from researching the issues affecting an organisation or the facts surrounding a particular campaign, it is vitally important for the public relations professional to examine in detail the communication process itself. This is done via a communication audit. In brief, a communication audit identifies those publics vital to an organisation's success. It investigates the scope of communication to determine whether all existing or potential publics are being covered. It examines their current attitudes and assesses whether or not work is required to crystallise, confirm or adjust those attitudes. It appraises critically the nature and quality of the communication between the organisation and its publics, looking carefully at the messages that are being relayed to see if they are what is required, their frequency and the techniques that are used to transmit them, as well as the effectiveness of the communication. It identifies communication gaps and unexploited opportunities, as well as the information needs of all the key publics. It also looks ahead by examining future information requirements and new methods of communication that should be used. An audit also pinpoints the resources and skills needed to run a successful programme or campaign, and whether or not these are available to an organisation.

To undertake an effective audit requires extensive research both within an organisation, with the whole range of personnel responsible for communication, and outside an organisation to investigate the opinions of those who are in contact with it.

Interpreting the findings

Collecting data is all very well and can be fun! But what do you do with all this data once you have it? At the risk of becoming boring, it is important to stress that analysing and interpreting data is a skilled job. All too often very simple analysis is done on very rich data. Obvious conclusions are drawn from simple statistics. It could be that 24 per cent of your sample said no to your questions, 26 per cent said yes, but 50 per cent said maybe. What does that mean? It could well be that enlightenment will come from using information from other parts of the survey. The golden rule is: once having paid good money for research, milk it for all it's worth, and you might need a professional to help you do that.

INVESTMENT IN RESEARCH PAYS – TWO CASES IN POINT

The point of doing research is to enable you to undertake your public relations programme more effectively. Identifying what the real issues are and the best way to go about executing your programme is, of course, vital to its success.

Research sometimes throws up the unexpected and drives you to conduct your programme in a way that you might not have anticipated. This is good news because if you conducted your programme in the way that you thought might be best, rather than the way that research dictates, you would end up wasting time, effort and money, and not achieve or at best only partially achieve your objectives. An example of how research guided a campaign in perhaps unexpected ways was the launch of Lego Mindstorms, handled by Manning, Selvage and Lee.

'From bricks to bytes': the launch of Lego Mindstorms

Mindstorms, or robotic Lego, was developed by the Lego Group to take the brand from toys to technology. The objective of the public relations campaign was to make Mindstorms a 'must have' for children and a 'must buy' for parents over the Christmas launch period. Research helped to define the child and parental audiences and to set communication objectives and messages for them.

Research with children

The first area of research was to identify very precisely the 'bullseye' target among children. Using the Youth Target Group Index, a database of 6,128 children aged between 7 and 18 researched by the British Market Research Bureau (BMRB), the consultancy identified 'tweens', that is 10- to 12- year-olds, as their main targets. This is the age at which children migrate from Lego bricks and become computer or video 'gamers'.

Lego Mindstorms was then piloted in the Media Lab at the Massachusetts Institute of Technology and it was discovered that children found the robotic potential of the product the most compelling thing. So this became the main communication message.

Qualitative research (interviews with 10- and 11-year-olds at school) indicated that 'tweens' would only trial the product if they saw that Mindstorms were adopted by and had the acceptance of their role models – typically hard-gaming older brothers and young men. Thus it became clear that 'tweens' needed to be reached via 'big brother' channels.

Research with parents

Qualitative research (in-depth interviews with parents) conducted by MLN Research on behalf of Manning, Selvage and Lee, identified that Mindstorms would have great appeal to parents if its educational value could be demonstrated. This was particularly important given that the product was perceived as expensive at £160 – very expensive if it were just a toy. Hence the communication message was 'educational value' and getting that across was the main focus of the campaign aimed at parents.

Key points about the research

From this pre-campaign research the following points can be noted:

- The consultancy used available research (Youth Target Group Index), specifically commissioned research (MLN Research with parents) and research conducted by themselves (among children at school) for the project. This mixed approach enabled them to combine specific expertise and existing materials as appropriate.
- The target group of children was pinpointed very precisely, which allowed a highly specific campaign to be developed.
- The product was piloted (pre-tested) with the target group and their interests were identified and then used in the campaign.
- The piloting was done at an internationally recognised centre of excellence for robotics, so the results themselves could be regarded as authentic. Furthermore, the reputation of MIT was also transferred to the product; the very fact that the trials were held there gave extra endorsement to the product.
- The interviews with the schoolchildren demonstrated that role-model approval was essential. Therefore, maybe surprisingly, the product was not aimed directly at the

target group (10- to 12-year-olds), but at their 'big-brothers', who acted as endorsing mediators to the target group.

- The research also provided specific message content for the communication that was to be directed at parents.

Based on this research, the public relations programme was rolled out in two distinct phases:

Phase one – 'Big Brother' adoption

To create a 'gotta have' feel for Mindstorms among 'tweens', the product needed to be raved about in the key media targeted, and read by 'big brother' (but often handed down to 'kid brother'). Beta versions of Mindstorms were presented to, and reviewed by, the key young-men's media as identified by TGI (Target Group Index, a database of 26,560 consumers researched by BMRB): *Stuff, T3* (Toys for the Boys' sections twice), *Maxim, Frontiers* and *Esquire*. Full-page reviews of Mindstorms appeared in the main computing and Internet magazines.

Phase two – parental acceptance

'Sleeper family' – Mindstorms was placed with a family to show how children were able to design and create their very own robots. This was offered as a testimonial on an exclusive basis to Sky TV.

'Cyber credentials' – a team from the Cybernetics Department at the University of Reading was recruited, and briefed to explore the robotic potential of the product. Exclusive rights were negotiated with BBC News 24 to film the robots being made and to interview Professor Kevin Warwick and his team prior to launch. Coverage was then rolled out to national and regional print and broadcast media.

Outcome and evaluation
Reach
- Young men – one in six males were reached.

- Parents – 50 per cent of parents were reached (57% of dads).

Message delivery
- Young men – 93 per cent of the articles stated that Mindstorms was a 'cool' or 'must have' product (research done by media-monitoring agency Metrica) and 71 per cent that it took the Lego brand into the future.
- Parents – 67 per cent of the articles/programmes cited the product's educational value.

Outcome
- Children – 21 per cent awareness of Mindstorms (23 per cent 10- to 11-year-olds), with one in two trialling (Carrick James New Brands Track, national survey among 7- to 15-year-olds).
- Parents – 36 per cent awareness of Mindstorms and 20,000 buying a set for Christmas (National Opinion Polls (NOP), parents of 10- to 16-year-olds were interviewed).

The verdict
- 'Lego Mindstorms is the best reason we can think of for having a kid' – *Maxim* magazine.
- 'Lego Mindstorms' was probably one of the most eagerly anticipated toys of the year and when the launch date finally arrived we had everyone from 8-year-olds to rocket scientists queuing up to buy it – the sales were phenomenal and we believe we sold more sets than anyone else'. Eva Saltman, Hamleys Marketing Manager.

Research can be used not only strategically to underpin a programme, but also as a specific tool for implementing a public relations campaign. Here the approach is quite overt. You come up front and say you have specifically researched a certain topic and you exploit the findings in the programme, either all at once or on a phased basis. You may make a virtue of undertaking the research regularly and announcing the results, for example the Halifax Bank research house prices and produces its house-price survey on a regular basis.

You may add credibility by enlisting the services of a well-known and respected research agency to undertake the work for you. Indeed, one of the more sure-fire media 'hooks' is to base a media campaign on research. The magical words are 'A survey has revealed...'. If that research touches on matters of public interest, it can serve a useful social purpose as well as obtaining publicity. The following example demonstrates how such research can be used.

'Rage against the machine' conducted by Firefly Communications for Compaq Computers Ltd

Compaq, the world's second-largest computer company, asked Firefly to create and implement a corporate public relations campaign to position it as the company dedicated to making information technology (IT) simpler. Compaq wanted to leave behind its stiff corporate image by appealing to the ordinary office worker and home PC owner. In other words, Compaq wanted both to appeal to its traditional business audience and to identify with new ones in the mainstream business and consumer sector. Compaq wanted these audiences to know that it was introducing a number of new products and services that would reduce the complexity of information technology. Furthermore, Compaq wanted to communicate that a PC is not a commodity but an important piece of equipment to get right. Therefore it was encouraging the use of an IT specialist to get the most out of asking consumers to buy equipment rather than hope for the best.

Strategy
Firefly proposed to launch a campaign based on independent

market research, highlighting a new phenomenon, computer rage. The subject was chosen because:

- it was built on an existing belief that IT is not simple and that for too long the IT industry has been leading the customers into thinking that it is;
- in order to make IT simpler for its customers, Compaq needed to understand end-users' frustrations;
- it provided a human-interest angle, which had not, to date, been explored;
- it provided the perfect platform for Compaq to communicate that it had introduced products and services addressing the problem of simplifying technology.

Action

The research was conducted by MORI. A survey questioned more than 1,250 workers in the UK to ascertain their views on whether IT was an asset or a burden, and the implications of the frustration they felt with IT. Of those who had their own PC at work, nearly half felt frustrated or stressed by the amount of time it takes to solve IT problems. Two in five blamed computer jargon for exacerbating the issue, while three-quarters of respondents who suffered daily problems with their PCs said that their colleagues swear at their monitors out of frustration.

Verbally abusing the PC is not the only response to IT stress; more than one in eight had seen their colleagues bully the IT department when things go wrong, while a quarter of under 25-years-old had seen peers kicking their computers. A similar number of respondents said that they had considered causing damage to their PC by deliberately pulling out its plug.

The survey found that computer rage has a business cost too. Nearly a quarter (23 per cent) of respondents said that their work was interrupted daily by computer crashes and other IT faults. Two in five who suffered daily breakdowns claimed that this delay has caused them to miss deadlines, while one in ten had felt like 'bad mouthing' their company to clients as well as friends because of frustration with the ineptness of their IT. This is despite the fact that one in six admitted that their PC problems are normally down to their own lack of knowledge and understanding.

The research also explored the role of the IT manager and how far those responsible for IT removed or contributed to the problems expressed. Nine out of ten respondents would not like the IT managers job and only 7 per cent said that their IT manager was given preferential treatment, despite the extremely stressful nature of the job. Of more concern was the fact that 75 per cent of respondents claimed that their IT manager couldn't sort out the problems that occurred, suggesting that IT vendors and employers alike should be taking more responsibility for delivering an IT compatible and stress-free atmosphere at work.

To provide the best possible news package for all media, the Firefly team included a video news release and a radio release, as well as paper-based and electronic format press materials. Regional research was also conducted to provide a local angle for the regional publications. To ensure interest in the story was widespread and the incidence of computer rage was highlighted as a genuine issue, it was essential to identify people who had become victims. Firefly sourced three who were prepared to speak to the media. The human element to the story, designed to bring the research to life, was backed up by the professional comment of Professor Robert J Edelmann, a leading psychologist on the causes of conflict at work.

Within Compaq itself, the different business units were asked to provide their own evidence of how their products and services reduced the complexity of IT. Firefly set up an e-mail address so that everyone could provide feedback. This helped to gel the campaign as a cross-Compaq campaign not tied to one particular area.

Exploitation of research

The results of the research revealed a new angle, showing how people react to computer rage in a variety of ways. The team pursued this angle through psychometric tests conducted by a psychologist, which produced the four personality profiles of 'Abusive Annie', 'Controlling Colin', 'Simmering Susan' and 'Analysing Alan'. These caricatures were based on the research and provided the basis for the helpline (see below), which added a tangible element to the research as well as providing interesting illustrations that were made available for publication.

To avoid the situation where the research might be covered, but without a mention of Compaq, the Firefly team suggested the inclusion of a computer rage helpline, which took the form of a series of recorded messages on the different personality types and way of dealing with their particular problem. This was a clever idea that was extensively used on radio and meant the press having to mention it as the 'Compaq Computer Helpline'.

Measurement

'Rage Against the Machine' achieved coverage on BBC One Business Breakfast, Channel 4 Big Breakfast, ITV Central News, BBC Breakfast News, BBC News 24, Channel 5 News, Bloomberg, Sky News Sky Sunrise – twice, Sky News Sky Business Report. The radio coverage was extensive, including a report on Radio 4 Today – twice, Radio 4 Debate and Radio 5 Breakfast and Late Night Live.

The campaign wholeheartedly met Compaq's objectives to reach a mass audience while promoting the 'IT made simple' message and the idea of a PC as more than a commodity. In seven months, it achieved nine pieces of television coverage, 43 radio hits, 10 Internet hits, and more than 30 printed pieces, including the *Financial Times*, *The Daily Telegraph*, *The Guardian*, *Daily Mail*, *The Sun*, *Evening Standard*, all the key IT titles in the UK, and

USA Today and the *New York Times* (which is quite unusual for a UK-based story).

5

Setting objectives

KNOWING WHERE YOU'RE GOING

Setting realistic objectives is absolutely vital if the programme or campaign that is being planned is to have direction and demonstrably achieve something.

One of the things that is rife in the public relations industry is over-promising. This applies to both in-house departments and consultancies. It comes partly from an eagerness to please, but largely from a lack of knowledge about what can actually be achieved.

Ultimately the aim of public relations is to influence attitudes and behaviour. You might want to encourage someone to buy your newly introduced furniture range, or keep their holdings in the company, or to speak up for the company when it is under attack. However, there are several steps along the way to influencing attitudes and it is only very occasionally that someone who is dedicated to opposing something or who has no particular opinion at all will suddenly become an ardent supporter.

ATTITUDE IS ALL IMPORTANT

According to American academics Cutlip, Center and Broom[1] public relations is about changing or neutralising hostile opinions, crystallising uninformed or latent opinions, or conserving favourable opinions.

Of course one of the things your research will have shown is exactly what the attitudes of the various publics or audiences are and this is vitally important when planning a programme. It is a much easier and less time-consuming job to reinforce favourable opinion that to neutralise hostile ones. In fact it may be that we would have to admit that it is impossible to neutralise ingrained opinions, particularly if they are based on deep-seated prejudice or fact.

So, how are the attitudes formed? All kinds of influences impact on us:

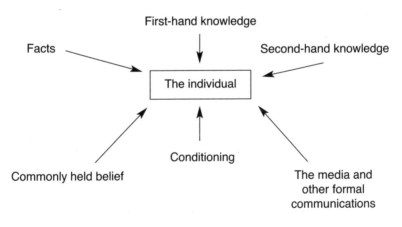

[1]Cutlip, S M, Centre, A H and Broom, G M (2000) *Effective Public Relations*, Prentice-Hall International, Upper Saddle River, New Jersey, 8th edn.

- *First-hand knowledge* is a very powerful attitude former. If you buy a car from a certain garage and the car itself, the sales and after-sales service has been excellent, you will have a favourable attitude towards them.
- *Second-hand knowledge* is also a strong influence, particularly if we gain that from a friend, trusted colleague or an authority of some kind. We may hear from them what a certain country is like and that knowledge, coupled with a good brochure, may persuade us to holiday there.
- *The media* is a potent influence, particularly if a topic is one of heightened public interest such as the concern over standards in public life. Companies also communicate via other formal methods such as annual reports, Web sites and product literature.
- *Conditioning* influences the way we look at everything we come into contact with. How we have been brought up, our education, religious beliefs, political views, our age, sex and social position are all part of the baggage we bring with us when thinking about any subject.
- Then there are *commonly held beliefs*. For example, we may believe, even though we may not own one or know anyone who does, that Aston Martins are superb cars or that Italian suits are especially well designed and made.
- *Facts* also affect our attitudes. Our knowledge that New Zealand is at the other side of the world will make us disbelieve anyone who says that they can cycle there in half an hour.

Usually attitudes are formed via a combination of all these factors. Some attitudes are very firmly fixed, like our view of the service we get from our bank, while other attitudes may be much more loosely held, for example our view of the Canadian government (in fact we may not have an attitude towards the Canadian government at all).

THE COMMUNICATION CHAIN

To set realistic objectives, apart from our understanding of what the attitudes of our various publics are, we also need to understand a little about the communication process. Assumptions along the lines of 'If I tell it loud and long and they hear it, eventually they'll believe it' are naive in the extreme. There are several models describing communication between individuals, groups and the main media. Just a few are outlined here to indicate the complexity of the subject.

Real communication involves the two-way exchange of information. However, many public relations practitioners in effect still believe that the one-way, linear communication model whose underlying principles were formulated by Shannon and Weaver[1] in 1949 is what happens in real life. The underlying pattern of the model is like this:

SENDER ———▶ MESSAGE ———▶ CHANNEL ———▶ RECEIVER

The idea is that the sender is active, the receiver is passive and that the message is fully understood. Furthermore, no distinction is drawn between communicating with individuals, groups, mass audiences or via third parties.

Communicating with individuals

The above model could apply to individuals, but what's missing is any notion of feedback. We need to know if our message has affected the receiver at all by changing or reinforcing attitudes, or making him or her behave in a particular way. A much more realistic model is the fairly well-known one shown in Figure 5.1.

The underlying principles behind this model were developed by Osgood and presented by Schramm[2] in 1954.

[1] Shannon, C and Weaver, W (1949) *The Mathematical Theory of Communication*, University of Illinois Press, Urbana, IL.
[2] Schramm, W (1954) How communication works, in *The Process and Effects or Mass Communication*, ed W Schramm, University of Illinois Press, Urbana, Illinois.

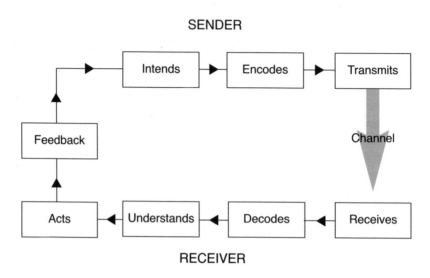

SENDER

RECEIVER

Figure 5.1   *The communication process model*

The sender intends to communicate and articulates or encodes that intention, bringing with him or her all the conditioning baggage mentioned before. He or she then chooses a channel through which to transmit the communication. This may be the spoken word, a page of text or a gesture, and the recipient receives that communication.

The actual transmission of information is fraught with danger. It may be that the message has associated channel noise. The radio may be crackly, the writing may be poorly laid out and hard to read or the Web site may be difficult to navigate. There may also be psychological noise. The sender might be using the wrong body language or the corporate message from the chief executive may be intimidating rather than informative. Then there is language noise, where the language itself can be misinterpreted. 'Do not cross while light is flashing' can mean do not cross when the light is flashing or do not cross until the light is flashing!

Having once received the message, the recipient then needs to decode it so that it can be understood. He or she also brings all his or her conditioning into the decoding equation. There is then normally some sort of action following on from the communication, which might be encoded or explicit. For example, this might be a simple grunt of recognition or a positive and vehement verbal rejection of the idea proposed, accompanied by a violent gesture. This action then has to be decoded by the receiver and acts as feedback. The loop is then closed, since the sender is looking for a reaction to the message that demonstrates communication has taken place. This allows the possibility of the sender adapting either his or her message or way of communicating, to help understanding and enhance communication. An important feature of this model is that the sender and receiver are seen as essentially equal and both are involved in encoding, decoding and interpreting. This, in fact, has led to some criticism of the model: it intimates a feeling of equality between the communicating parties. However, observation demonstrates this is not the case, there are sometimes large differences in motivation, power, resources and time between the participants.

More recent models of communication have emphasised the cyclical nature of the process. Rogers and Kincaid[1] developed the 'convergence' model (see Figure 5.2), in which the participants in communication give and receive information and explore their understanding of it to the point where there is such a level of mutual understanding (which does not need to be complete) that further exchanges are not necessary.

The models so far are particularly applicable to one-to-one, interpersonal communication, where there can be relatively easy checks on understanding and where there is feedback, for example, one-to-one briefings of analysts. They are less suitable as descriptions of what happens between organisations and groups or between organisations and mass audi-

[1]Rogers, E M and Kincaid, D L (1981) *Communication Networks: Towards a new Paradigm for Research*, The Free Press, New York.

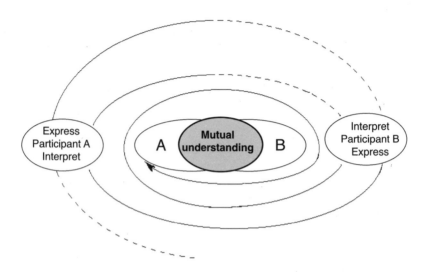

Figure 5.2   *The convergence model of communication*

Reprinted with the kind permission of The Free Press, a division of Simon & Schuster Inc, from *Communication Networks: Toward a new paradigm for research* by Everett M Rogers and D Lawrence Kincaid. Copyright ©1981 by The Free Press

ences or groups reached through a third party such as the media, where there can be relatively little feedback or direct personal interaction.

Communicating with groups

There are several models available describing communication with groups; one that is quite widely accepted in public relations circles is the 'co-orientation model'.[1] This is particularly

---

[1]First proposed by J M McLeod and S H Chaffee (1977) in 'Interpersonal approaches to communication research', *American Behavioural Scientist*, 16, pp 469–500, but since then refined and applied specifically to public relations.

applicable where the organisation is involved in a genuine dialogue – two-way, interactive communication in which the organisation is prepared to change its position to accommodate its public. It is not applicable where the organisation is just giving out pure information or is undertaking a propaganda exercise. Here the sender/message/channel/receiver or the communication process models are more applicable.

Without going into the fine detail of the co-orientation model, its principal features are accuracy, understanding and agreement. An example will illustrate the idea. Suppose a company wishes to set up a plastic recycling plant in a town. It thinks it will provide employment, stimulate the local economy and serve a laudable 'green' cause. Local residents, however, may see this development as bringing heavy lorries to the district, polluting the air and taking up space that could be used for much-needed housing. Each party may have a quite inaccurate perception of the views of the other; they may not understand each other's point of view and they certainly don't agree.

The company, realising that there is a potential major problem, holds a meeting with residents so that both sides can explain their point of view and some sort of rapprochement can be reached. They co-orient themselves by jointly compromising and coming up with a mutually agreed solution – at least that is the theory and the aspiration!

Communicating with mass audiences or via the mass media

When we are dealing with mass audiences there are many receivers and it is impossible to influence people in a uniform way. People select information depending on their various states of knowledge or their predisposition. Receivers talk to each other, they are influenced by opinion leaders and so on. This recognition has led to the development of the two-step communication model[1], where the information is received by key 'gatekeepers' (normally opinion leaders), who further interpret for the mass audience.

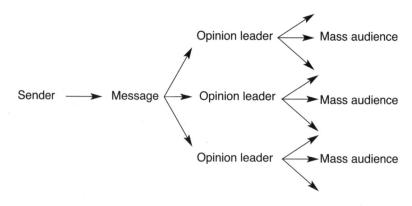

Thus, for example, if a public relations practitioner sends out a press release, the targeted journalists perform the role of opinion leaders and interpret the information on behalf of their readers. Again, some uniformity of interpretation is assumed.

In reality this model is simplistic too. People receive information from all kinds of sources and this often bypasses the opinion leader. Communication is multi-faceted, multi-step and multi-directional.[2]

All this communication is overlaid with individual and group attitudes, psychological variables, channel noise, feedback from various sources and the knowledge base of all those involved. Little wonder, then, that communication with mass audiences is an immensely complex and open-ended business.

---

[1]First proposed by E Katz and P F Lazarsfeld in *Personal Influence*, Free Press, Glencoe.
[2]See Windahl, S, Signitzer, B with Olson, J (1991) *Using Communication Theory*, Sage, London, for further explanation.

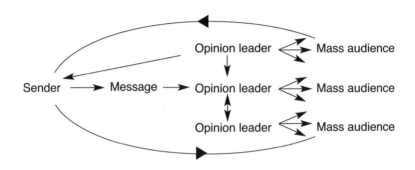

COMMUNICATING ON THE INTERNET

All the models discussed so far have attempted to describe communication using traditional, well-established methods. Internet communication breaks most of the rules. Whole books have been written on e-PR and it is advisable to read them to get a thorough grasp of the implications for public relations practice. While there isn't space here to go into great detail about Internet public relations, a number of salient points need to be borne in mind when running campaigns that are exclusively or partially Internet-based.

Unique properties of the Internet

- Once the message is out, the sender loses control. The Internet has 'agency' in a way that no other medium has. It is a channel of communication, but a channel that is used to transform, alter, correct, attack and/or support a message in a unique way. A printed newspaper story remains the same – set in type. On the Net, messages can be taken over by anyone and transformed in real time. It is not a neutral channel.

- The Internet is both transitory (a swift, immediately deleted e-mail response to a current question) and virtually permanent (a Web site can remain on-line, accessible and unchanged for years).
- It is not time constrained. A message left in a newsgroup, or sent by e-mail, can be responded to at any time. A Web site can be visited at a visitor's convenience.
- It provides a unique medium in which communities and groups of communities can form, reform, transform and dissolve.
- It is location free. Access is available as easily 12,000 miles away as in the next office. Furthermore, it recognises no geographical, social or political boundaries.
- It is virtually cost-free once set-up has been completed. Cybercafés and use of employers' machines mean that anyone can be a communicator. Home machines are relatively cheap.
- It provides one-to-one (e-mail), one-to-many (newsgroups and personal Web sites), many-to-many (chat, newsgroups, etc) and many-to-one (e-mail) all at the same time.
- The speed of the medium and the quantity of material that can be accessed (including images and sound) is unprecedented.
- Internet users have a different mindset. They have power because they can form and reform as different communities with great speed. They can be anonymous or have a different on-line personality and act differently as a result. This has both an on-line and an off-line impact for the individual concerned.

Communication implications of the Internet

Referring to the earlier discussion on public relations theories leads to a number of conclusions:

- Transparent, two-way, pro-active public relations is the only sensible way to operate: there are too many other sources of information to permit any alternative. In addition, being seen to be a useful information resource and providing transparent access is regarded as a positive.

- Publics must be seen as collecting around issues rather than as homogeneous blocks such as 'customers'. Even where there are homogeneous groups such as at chatrooms for City analysts, the discussion is normally issues based. Furthermore, because issues can remain on Web sites or discussion groups for prolonged periods, the choice of when to react is in the hands of publics. They can re-emerge at any stage, maybe years later, as different groups of people gather round the issue and form a 'new' public. (See Chapter 6 for more detail on issues-based publics.)

- The Internet is ideally suited to *active* and *aware* publics (who may become active if they could acquire additional information from the medium itself), who are information-seekers. They are potentially the greatest friends of an organisation as well as its greatest 'problems'. (For a full explanation of active and aware publics, see Chapter 6.)

- The thought to action continuum desired by organisational communicators can be reinforced or broken by users accessing alternative information sources, many of which may be unknown to the organisation.

- This continuum will be time-contracted, as information for decision-making is readily and swiftly available. Prompts to action in support of or opposition to an organisation can be stimulated when a user is part of a like-minded and supportive community (witness the two demonstrations against capitalism in the City of London and the demonstration against the World Trade Organisation in Seattle, which were both organised through the Internet).

- Lack of information from organisations is a potentially serious problem because there will be several, readily accessible alternative sources, not all of which may be supportive. Not providing information is regarded as secretive and in itself can create an issue around which a public can gather.

- The Internet changes the power relationships between stakeholder networks because smaller interest groups can present their case as well as large organisations and can interact directly with other stakeholders. The Internet is an activist's friend.
- Individual opinions have equal weight, no one is more important than anyone else. Opinions are formed in a different way, usually by other Net users who are of the same Internet peer group or from trusted alternative sources such as BBC Online. The traditional opinion formers, for example the off-line media and community leaders, are less influential.
- Communication is direct, without the mediation of, say, journalists or other traditional opinion formers, although some users gather material from other Internet sources to support their argument to good effect.
- It is essentially a 'pull' or 'demand' medium. There are limited opportunities to 'push' information without users seeking it. Portal advertising could be regarded as 'push', but its efficacy is open to question (as indicated by the low advertising charges). Practitioners will find themselves increasingly providing demand-led information, such as responding to e-mail and Web site enquiries, and will need to rethink their roles in these terms.
- With their knowledge of stakeholders and their management, public relations professionals are uniquely placed to be the knowledge managers for their organisations. Indeed, there have been calls for a new role for the public relations professional at this higher level. They are neither technicians nor managers, but communication executives who will be regarded as the peers of the highest executives in the organisation.

HOW 'RECEIVERS' USE INFORMATION

Work in the communication field in the late 1950s speculated that we seek out information that is in tune with our own attitudes and resist messages that conflict with them. More recent work indicates that people select information because it is relevant to them, not because it reinforces their views. So, if you buy a new personal computer you might find out a lot about the various products available before choosing the one you eventually buy. Having bought the computer you then continue to seek out information about it, not to confirm your choice, but because you want to find out as much as possible about your new machine so you can exploit it to the full.

The key thing is that the receiver is not passive but does something with the information, even if that it is just to store it away for future reference. Many public relations practitioners want to believe in the Domino Theory[1] of the effect of communication.

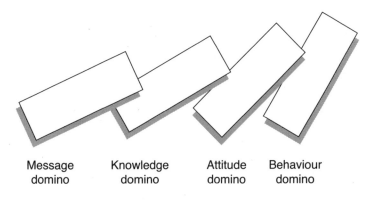

Message domino   Knowledge domino   Attitude domino   Behaviour domino

This is reflected in early marketing theory which was based on the AIDA model. First of all people become Aware of an idea or product or service but have little knowledge about it.

[1]Grunig, J E and Hunt, T (1984) *Managing Public Relations*, Holt, Rinehart and Winston, New York.

Then they develop an Interest and seek out more information. Then they become persuaded of the benefits of the idea or product or service and develop a Desire to buy it. Finally they show their support by taking Action and buying the product or service.

Sometimes this simple progression is fine, but often it is not. In fact, Grunig and Holt state that the chances of someone progressing through the dominos from the point where, the message is received to behaving in a desired way are 4 in 10,000. An audience or public might learn about an organisation and form a negative rather than a positive attitude, or they might develop an attitude but not take the desired action.

The portrayal of wars and famines often engenders strong sympathy in the minds of television viewers and newspaper readers, but they might not make a charitable donation as a result. There is certainly no proven causal link between people thinking about something, forming an attitude and then acting in a predictable way. Public relations people may provide and present in an attractive manner all the information an individual needs to think or act in a particular way. However, the way those individuals form their attitudes and behave is usually very specific to them and their particular situation, and is not entirely predictable.

Furthermore, people are very adept at holding incompatible beliefs and these might change. For example, individuals may be vociferous supporters of measures to combat environmental pollution, but may own a car. They will therefore argue differently depending on the situation they are talking about. One thing is very clear; if someone is very firmly of a particular opinion and acts to support it, it will be very difficult to persuade him or her to a different point of view. It is not that communication has no effect, but we do need to know where our public or audience stands before we can construct realistic objectives. Just giving people lots of positive information will not necessarily change their attitudes or behaviour. The leverage points (points of weakness in their argument or strength in ours) have to be identified and worked upon in order to make productive shifts in attitude or behaviour. If there are no leverage points which can be worked on persuasively, the argument is lost from the start.

SETTING REALISTIC OBJECTIVES

Bearing all this in mind, then, we can now look at setting achievable objectives. Objectives are usually set at one of three levels:

- *Awareness* – getting your target public to think about something and trying to promote a level of under-standing. These are often called *cognitive* (thinking) objectives. An example could be the government wishing to make you aware of a change in tax rates.
- *Attitudes and opinions* – getting your target public to form a particular attitude or opinion about a subject. These are often called *affective* objectives. An example could be a pressure group wanting your moral support for or against abortion.
- *Behaviour* – getting your target public to act in a desired way. These are often called *conative* objectives. An example could be a local police force using the radio to ask people to stay away from a major accident site.

It would be easy to get depressed given all the factors that seem to militate against you achieving anything substantial, but this is not the case at all. There are three things that are very much in your control.

- You can choose the desired effect of the communications. So if you are introducing a new or difficult idea, you might work at the awareness levels first; you don't have to try to obtain a behavioural response immediately!

- You can choose who the target publics are and, further-more, you can enlist the help of those individuals or groups within those target publics who are already favourably disposed towards you or who could be readily enlisted (more of this in Chapter 6).
- The persuasion doesn't need to be all one way. As stated several times, the organisation can change too and some-times relatively small changes in organisational attitude or behaviour can result in major positive effects on your target public.

The principle to remember is that it is a much larger and more difficult task to get someone to act than it is to get them to think about something, thus most public relations objectives will be at the cognitive (thinking) and affective (attitude or opinion-forming) levels rather than at the conative (behav-ioural) level. So the kinds of objectives public relations programmes might have could be to:

- create awareness;
- promote understanding;
- overcome misunderstanding or apathy;
- inform;
- develop knowledge;
- displace prejudice;
- encourage belief;
- confirm or realign a perception;
- act in a particular way.

In the Manning, Selvage and Lee campaign for Mindstorms quoted in Chapter 4, the objectives of the programme were very clear: to create awareness of the fact that Mindstorms had educational value (a key leverage point – parents are prepared to spend money on their children's education); to demonstrate that the product had credibility with older role models; to inform parents and children of the product's cyber potential'; and to get them to buy it.

EIGHT GOLDEN RULES OF OBJECTIVE SETTING

There are seven imperatives that must be borne in mind when setting objectives:

- *Ally to organisational objectives*. Public relations programmes and campaigns must support corporate objectives, otherwise effort will be dissipated on interesting but essentially trivial and tactical work. If a corporate objective is a major repositioning of the company in its market, then the public relations effort must be directed to supporting that.
- *Set public relations objectives*. Again it is a tendency of public relations professionals to set objectives that public relations cannot deliver. It is not reasonable to say that public relations should increase sales by 20 per cent. That depends on the salesforce. It is reasonable to say that presentations should be made to 50 per cent of our key retailers to tell them of our new product lines and to try them. It may well be that as a result sales do increase by 20 per cent – but it is outside our control to promise this.
- *Be precise and specific*. Objectives need to be sharp. To create awareness is not good enough. Creating awareness of what, to whom, when and how needs to be clearly spelt out.
- *Do what is achievable*. It is better to set modest objectives and hit them, than to aim for the sky and miss. Wherever possible evaluate the likely benefits of ideas and pre-test or pilot schemes. If a major part of the programme is to contact all investors to inform them of a particular development, you must be sure you can do it within the Stock Market rules.
- *Quantify as much as possible*. Not all objectives are precisely quantifiable, but most are. If you aim to contact particular audience groups say how many. Quantifying objectives makes evaluation much easier.

- *Work to a timescale.* Know when you are going to deliver, then you can pace yourself or bring in help as required.
- *Work within budget.* This goes without saying. It is no good claiming to be creative and therefore not interested in money. A good planner and manager knows exactly how much things will cost, and will run budget tracking programmes.
- *Work to a priority list.* Public relations people always have too much to do and they could extend their list of activities indefinitely. Know what your priorities are and stick to them religiously. If you do have to work on non-prioritised work, make sure you let your superiors know the consequences of their demands. Prioritising objectives enables you to see where the major effort is to be focused.

Remember the SMART acronym for objectives: Stretching, Measurable, Achievable (given other activities), Realistic (you have the resources to achieve them) and Timebound.

Examples of workable objectives are as follows:

Corporate	Inform 10 targeted investors of reasons for management buyout before the AGM and obtain their support.
Trade:	Ensure 50 top dealers attend annual dealers' conference.
Consumer:	Increase levered editorial coverage of service by 20 per cent over 18 months.
Employees:	Maximise branch acceptance of corporate clothing by December (90 per cent is target for acceptance).
Community:	Double job applications from local school-leavers within 2 years.

CONSTRAINTS ON OBJECTIVES

Of course it would be nice to plan without any form of constraint, but there are usually a number of factors that have to be given careful regard. These are either internally or externally generated.

Internal constraints

- *Who should do the job?* The capabilities of the people assigned to the task need careful assessment. Are they able to carry it out? If not, will this mean that the demands of the task will have to be limited? Alternatively, is it possible to enlist the help of other people such as a public relations consultancy? Do you have enough people for the task? Again can extra hands be drafted in or will the scope of the task need to be reduced?
- *How much will it cost?* No one has an open-ended budget so what are the effects on your prioritised programme of any budgetary constraints? What can you leave out if necessary?
- *When does it need to happen?* Sometimes an internal timetable will require that the public relations task has to be carried out at a certain time, for example, the announcement of a major company restructure or the introduction of a new process.
- *Who makes the decisions?* Are the public relations professionals able to decide on the appropriate courses of action or is the power elsewhere, such as with a marketing director?
- *Is the support in place?* Is there the right administrative back-up and physical resources such as faxes, Internet access and video conferencing, to support the programme?

External constraints

- *Who are you trying to reach?* What is the range of publics or audiences? How many are there? What is their geographical spread? What about their socio-economic grouping?
- *What are the socio-cultural differences?* What are the different media conventions in the various countries you are operating in? What social and cultural differences have to be observed?
- *What infrastructure support is there?* What facilities such as telephone or access to computers are available?
- *Time frames?* Are their certain calendar dates such as Christmas or Bonfire Night that have to be met? What about other key events such as the Motor Show or the Ideal Home Exhibition?

STRATEGIC AND TACTICAL OBJECTIVES

Objectives can, of course, apply to whole programmes or individual projects. They can also operate at two levels, the strategic and the tactical.

The example below shows how an issue that an organisation faces translates into objectives at both the strategic and tactic level.

ISSUE	STRATEGIC OBJECTIVE	TACTICAL OBJECTIVE
Company seen as backward	Position as company that produces innovative products	Promote this product as innovative
Company not seen as contributor to community	Position as company that takes public responsibility seriously	Promote company-sponsored recycling scheme in community
Company not seen as caring employer	Position as company committed to employees	Promote women-returners scheme

The setting of good, realistic objectives is fundamental to the success of public relations plans and campaigns. They provide the whole basis of the programme by clearly setting down what the key achievements must be. They become the rationale behind the strategy, set the agenda for the actions to be taken and provide the benchmark for evaluation further down the road. When put into practice, they also guide management decisions, such as where to cut resources if necessary, or where to expand the budget and put in extra effort.

The temptation to over-promise must be resisted. That is not so say that public relations practitioners should set themselves soft targets, they should be as rigorous as any other business area. They must, however, recognise the complexity of the communication process, and be realistic about what shifts in attitude and behaviour can be achieved.

Programmes that aim to produce radical shifts in attitude and behaviour usually take a great deal of time and are bound initially to meet with a limited amount of success. There are, of course, exceptions to break the rule, and these are often triggered by a crisis or the creation of a 'hot issue' that is fuelled by the media. Generally speaking, however, the most successful programmes start from the point where the audiences are, and attempt to make incremental shifts which, over a period of time, can be seen to have made considerable progress. The reputations of our best companies have taken considerable time to build. Public relations activity is to do with building reputations, too, and that is a slow and painstaking business.

6

Knowing the publics and messages

WHO SHALL WE TALK TO AND WHAT SHALL WE SAY?

Having answered the question 'Where am I going?' by setting achievable, measurable objectives, the next question to ask is 'Who shall I talk to?'

By undertaking research for the proposed programme you will already have an analysis of the attitudes of each of the audiences that relate to the organisation. Now these audiences or publics need to have a priority order put on them. Sometimes the priorities are fairly obvious. If you want to launch a new product, the primary audiences are going to be existing and potential customers. However, sometimes the latter grouping is more difficult. Maybe you need to begin to speak to groupings with whom you have had little or nothing to do. If you are a private company seeking a stock market listing then you will need to speak to the City, financial journalists and potential investors, and you will have to begin from scratch.

There are groupings of publics that are fairly common to most organisations. These are shown in Figure 6.1.

Again it is a common failing of public relations practitioners that they perform a rather simple and crude chopping up of the publics that organisations have. They believe that a particular grouping contains individuals who all act in the same way.

In Chapter 5, when we discussed objective setting, we saw how radical shifts in attitude and behaviour are very difficult to achieve. It is vital therefore that we understand what can be achieved with particular audiences or publics and the different sub-sections within them.

WHAT IS PUBLIC OPINION?

It is worth spending a little time discussing public opinion since what we are trying to do in public relations is shift the balance of opinion of the various publics we interact with in favour of our organisation. Public opinion can be broadly regarded as the prevalent view held by the majority of people. It is against this background that our work with particular publics takes place. One definition of public opinion is as follows:

> Public opinion represents a consensus, which emerges over time, from all the expressed views that cluster around an issue in debate, and that this consensus exercises power.[1]

[1] Cutlip, S M, Center, A H and Broom, G M (2000) *Effective Public Relations*, Prentice-Hall, Upper Saddle River, New Jersey, 8th edn.

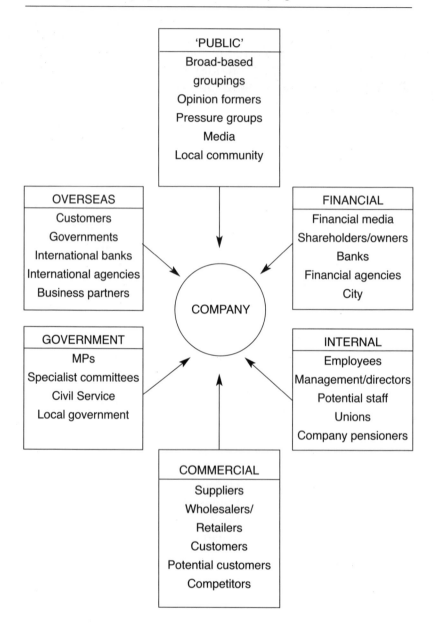

Figure 6.1 *Publics common to most organisations*

Public opinion works two ways: it is both a cause and effect of public relations activity. Public opinion, strongly held, affects management decisions. For example, increasing concerns for the environment have affected the motor and furniture industries. Noxious emissions from cars have been cut and trade in non-replantable hardwoods is frowned on. Public relations practitioners publicise the fact that their organisations care for the environment.

On the other hand, a stated objective of many public relations programmes is to affect public opinion, often by mounting a media relations campaign. The commonly held view is that public opinion is 'what is in the media' and if we can change what the media says, public opinion will also change. However, as we saw in Chapter 4, implanting an opinion does not always change behaviour.

Most people have opinions on most things, you only have to ask them. The fear of many public relations practitioners is that these opinions could be drawn together and focused by the media against their organisation. The hope is by getting an organisation's message out, mass opinion will be supportive. Thus many public relations programmes adopt a scattergun approach, spreading very general messages to very broad publics.

Research in America[1] has found that only 33 per cent of Americans aged between 18 and 29 and 48 per cent of those aged between 30 and 49 enjoy keeping up to date with the news. (This increased to 68 per cent for those over 65.)

This apparent lack of interest can be very easily explained. Most people have neither the time nor the energy to be involved in everything. They are selective and devote time to those things that they are involved in, and where they feel they can make a contribution.

Uniform public opinion occurs very occasionally and well-informed public opinion occurs even more rarely.

---

[1] Pew Research Center Biennial News Consumption Survey, 1998.

The media do not determine what people think, however they do provide a platform for discussing issues and they can reinforce the 'public' view if a particular issue catches the imagination.

However, what appears to be a small proportion of the total population (for example students) concerned with a particular issue (Third World indebtedness) can be a large group when all banded together and can affect the mission of a business (eg the UK banks).

Opinions are very interesting phenomena and can operate at different levels. Asked for a view of something in the news, most people will offer an opinion. That might be superficial and not always thought-through. These views might be called perceptions. At a deeper level people may have an opinion about a particular issue such as hanging, which has been well thought through and for which they can produce arguments. They can be said to have a particular attitude towards that subject. At an even deeper level attitudes can turn into forms of behaviour. At the most extreme, this could take the form of direct action which could be against the law, such as some of the activities of the more militant animal rights groups.

People can hold two conflicting opinions at the same time. For example, they might think animal experiments are wrong in general, but also believe that certain types of drugs should be tested on animals before being used on human beings.

TYPES OF PUBLICS

James Grunig[1] defines four sorts of publics:

- *Non-publics*, which are groups that neither are affected by nor affect the organisation. For example, a retailer based in southern England will have no effect on and will not be

---

[1]Grunig, J E and Hunt, T (1984) *Managing Public Relations*, Holt, Rinehart & Winston, New York.

affected by publics based in Edinburgh. Broadly speaking, these publics can be ignored and are often not even identified.

● *Latent publics*, which are groups that face a problem as a result of an organisation's actions, but fail to recognise it. For example, a haulage company expanding its business may increase local traffic levels, yet the local residents may be unaware of this.

● *Aware publics*, which are groups that recognise that a problem exists. In our haulage company example, the local residents may read a press story that tells them about the expansion.

● *Active publics*, which are groups that do something about the problem. For example, local residents may blockade the haulage company's gates.

Active publics can be further broken down into three categories:

● *All-issue publics* are active on all issues affecting an organisation. For instance, that public might be opposed to the organisation in principle and try to disrupt all its activities. An example of this is the anti-nuclear lobby, which will oppose all the work of any company involved in handling nuclear material, even that which may be non-nuclear related.

● *Single-issue publics* are active on one issue or a small set of issues – for example the Save the Whale campaign. They might not be opposed to an organisation per se, but will oppose any activity that is contrary to their view on that particular issue. In fact they may be broadly supportive of an organisation, but totally opposed to one particular activity, such as giving advantageous share options to directors.

● *Hot-issue publics* are those involved in an issue that has broad public support and usually gets extensive media coverage. An example of this would be the public support for Greenpeace over the issue of the disposal of the Brent Spar oil platform.

There are also what Grunig calls:

- *Apathetic publics,* which are publics basically unconcerned by all problems and are effectively not a public at all. However, some theorists would argue that these publics are a grouping that should concern public relations practitioners – everyone has the potential to become interested in an issue.

When an organisation or its publics behave in such a way that the other is affected, then a problem or issue arises. Publics, Grunig argues, are created by specific situations and the problems or opportunities they cause. There is no such thing as a 'general' situation or a 'general' public.

Responses to issues depend very much on individual circumstances. Why is it, with the best of intentions, people sometimes just don't get round to writing that cheque for that good cause?

Grunig provides some explanations about when and how people communicate and when communications aimed at particular publics are likely to be effective. He says that there are three main factors that need to be taken into account:

- *Problem recognition* – In essence, people won't think about a situation unless they believe that something needs to be done about it, ie they have a problem.

    If you have a group of people who are actively seeking information about a situation, they are more likely to become 'aware' or 'active' publics than those who just passively receive the information without making any effort. So the communications professional will need to identify those 'information seekers', provide them with what they need and enter into a dialogue; otherwise, they may go elsewhere and obtain less than supportive material.

In our example of the haulage company that is expanding, the public relations professional would need to identify those people who perceive the company's expansion plans as problematic, find out those who want information and provide an appropriate channel of communication; otherwise, they might go to an anti-traffic lobby for advice and information.

Those people who recognise that they have a problem often seek information as a precursor to action; so the provision of information is vital.

- *Constraint recognition* – This is the extent to which people perceive that there are constraints on their ability to act in the way they want. So if people think there is little or nothing they can do about the expansion of a haulage company, they will probably not want information about it. If, however, they believe that they can do something, they will communicate with all kinds of organisations to get information and advice.

While problem recognition and constraint recognition often determine what information a public will want about a situation, the third factor usually affects their behaviour.

- *Level of involvement* – This is how connected someone feels to a situation. So if people live next door to the haulage company, they may feel very involved because they are likely to be most affected by the increase in traffic. Those four streets away may not be as affected, so may not become actively involved, even if they recognise the problem and think they could do something about it.

So from the public relations professional's point of view, those people who are highly involved in an issue usually have strong problem recognition and minimal constraints. They are likely to be most active and to demand most information. Those not involved or who face high levels of constraints may be aware publics, but are unlikely to become active unless they become involved or their constraints are removed. Their situation needs to be monitored so as to avoid any surprise when they do become active.

The approach of Grunig allows us to define publics for organisations from two angles:

- First of all, a public is defined by considering very carefully exactly who will be affected by the policies and activities of that organisation.
- Second, by monitoring the environment it is possible to identify those publics that have particular interests in specific issues, whose opinion and behaviour will significantly affect the activities of the organisation.

This apparently theoretical approach is useful, since if an organisation identifies its issued-based publics it will pinpoint those who are likely to be the activists on any particular issue. This is particularly important when dealing with Internet communities, which we have seen (Chapter 5) form around issues.

From this it is clear that active publics are the most likely to use information from public relations programmes as a prompt for their behaviour. They will only be a proportion of the targeted population; however, it is important to identify them since communication effort should be focused on them.

A further note of caution is needed. Grunig says that if you choose attitudes or behaviour as your objective (remembering that you will probably have worked on awareness already), don't expect to affect more than 20 per cent of the target group and don't forget that some of these will be negative in their response. The importance in researching the attitudes of the various publics, what they think of the organisation and how they act so that we can understand and communicate more effectively, cannot be overemphasised.

It is, of course, eminently sensible to put together the traditional way of segmenting publics into consumers, employees, etc, with Grunig's approach. The broader categories can be analysed for those subgroups that are likely to be active, aware and latent. It brings a very potent communication perspective and helps prioritise the actions of the communicator.

SO WHAT ABOUT THE MEDIA?

Earlier we played down the role of the media in influencing public opinion, but it is obvious that it does have a powerful role in our lives. Here are some general observations.

The media are more likely to create a public when the information is negative. People react against child abuse or over-inflated executive pay. If the coverage is extensive and the topic catches the imagination it is possible that a hot-issue public could be created.

Hot-issue publics often react to the thing of the moment without necessarily thinking things through carefully, and once media interest dies down, so does theirs. However, if an organisation handles a hot issue badly it could turn hot-issue publics into longer-term active ones by forcing them to think more deeply about the issues concerned. The growing support for 'natural foods' is a case in point.

Media campaigns to promote companies are most likely to reach active publics who positively seek out any information about the organisation they are interested in.

THE IMPLICATIONS FOR TARGETING PUBLICS

The implications of all this are fairly obvious. Don't waste time on publics that are not interested in what you are doing or saying, but always keep an eye on them just in case. If a public is important to you, but inactive (for example, inactive members in a shareholder syndicate), you will have to be very imaginative in attracting their attention to the information you want to give them. Clever writing, good creative photography, eye-catching and relevant headlines will need to be employed. Active publics are the 'communicators' friend'. They positively seek out and want to understand information. It is possible to keep a low profile with them; however, if you don't supply information, they will seek it from elsewhere and being active it could be that they will act against you as well as for you.

Don't expect changes in attitude and behaviour from huge numbers of your publics. Only a proportion of your active and aware publics are likely to respond. However, they can act as catalysts for change and their power should not be underestimated.

HOW TO SELECT YOUR PUBLICS

Disregard the 'general' public, it does not exist as far as public relations is concerned.

The easiest way to categorise publics is to move from the general to the particular. First of all define broad categories to identify their connections with the organisation. Divide these broad categories into particular groups. This could be done on the basis of geography or the level of activity likely from the group, or on the power and influence of that group.

Prioritise the groups. An example is given in Figure 6.2 (the groupings are very broad, but the principle holds).

Table 6.1 *Proportioning out the public relations effort to different publics*

Grouping	Percentage of communication effort required	
Corporate		25
Shareholders (active)	10	
Shareholders (latent)	2	
Government ministers (active)	4	
Government ministers (aware)	3	
Opposition front bench (active)	3	
Opposition front bench (aware)	1	
Senior civil servants	2	
Customers		25
ABC1 householders (current purchasers)	10	
ABC1 householders (potential)	5	
Retail shops (active)	7	
Retail shops (new)	3	
Employees		20
Executives	3	
Supervisors	7	
Shopfloor workers	7	
Trade union leaders	3	
Community		15
Neighbours	4	
Community leaders	5	
Schools		
Headteachers	2	
PTA	2	
Governors	2	
Suppliers		9
Raw materials		
major suppliers	6	
minor suppliers	3	
Services		6
major suppliers	4	
minor suppliers	2	

The overall level of activity is likely to be limited by budget.

Identify the gatekeepers or the leaders of the active groups who are likely to interpret information for others or act as catalysts for action. Remember that individuals or groups can belong to more than one category so there needs to be identification and monitoring of the crossovers to ensure that publics are treated equitably, and so that conflicting messages are not transmitted.

WHAT SHALL WE SAY?

The nature of particular messages will of course vary, depending on the nature of the individual campaign of which they are a part. However, every public relations plan or campaign needs to have a set of messages that forms the main thrust of the communication. These messages need to be clear, concise and readily understood.

Messages are important for two main reasons. First of all they are an essential part of the attitude-forming process. If publics play back to the originator the message that the originator has initiated, it is a clear indication (a) that the message has been received and (b) that the message has been taken on board and is in some way being used. That may be just as a part of the thinking process, or it may permeate as far as actions.

The second reason messages are important is that they demonstrate the effectiveness of the communication. They are an essential part of the evaluation process. If distinct messages are utilised directly by the press, or if they are repeated in research such as attitude surveys, that clearly shows the messages have been assimilated. It is quite a small step then to see what actions have been taken as a result of the communication.

Messages are often underestimated, but they are vitally important and can't just be flung together or applauded because they are clever. They are the point of contact between an organisation and its publics in communication terms. They are what are 'given' by the organisation and 'received' by the public and vice versa. Messages and the way they are conveyed are the starting point of the thinking, attitude or behavioural change that the organisation is seeking. Badly done, they can be the end point too.

DETERMINING THE MESSAGES

There are four steps in determining messages:

- *Step one* is to take existing articulated perceptions. For example, it may be that your organisation's products are regarded as old-fashioned and this has been identified in earlier research.
- *Step two* is to define what shifts can be made in those perceptions. If, in fact, your products have been substantially upgraded you need to say that loud and clear.
- *Step three* is to identify elements of persuasion. The best way to do this is to work on the basis of fact. You might be making major investments in upgrading your plant. It could be that there has been a series of new technology initiatives. Maybe you have won an innovation award recently. These are all facts that falsify the view that your products are old-fashioned.
- *Step four* is to ensure that the messages are credible and deliverable through public relations. It may be that advertising or direct mail should be enlisted to put across a public relations message.

In its campaign to reposition ICL (which has provided cash tills and National Lottery ticket dispensers) as a voice of authority in the retail services sector, Paragon Communications used research-based market-leading reports of technology in the retail services sector to demonstrate how ICL was making the running on the technology front. The message was clear. ICL understood and provided the right technology solutions for the sector. As a result, in two years ICL moved from 17 per cent of retailers viewing the company as market leader to 38 per cent holding that view.

Messages can be general in nature. Sometimes they have an overall corporate thrust. Advertising pay-off lines or company straplines such as Peugeot's 'The lion goes from strength to strength' are a good example. The organisation's message is that it is healthy, growing and successful.

These general messages are often backed up by very specific sub-messages which may pinpoint a particular piece of information or a specific service that an organisation wants to put across.

For example, the Royal Mail has a main message on its commitment to the local community.

It also has various sub-messages to illustrate the main message 'Royal Mail cares about the community'. Among them are, 'Royal Mail makes charitable donations', 'Royal Mail is a sponsor of events, organisations, people and/or initiatives which contribute positively to the community' and Royal Mail 'is an ethical and responsible company'.

It is, of course, important that messages do not conflict as people can belong to more than one public. It is perfectly feasible for there to be differences in nuance, but the overall thrust of the messages must be in broad sympathy with each other.

HOW THE MESSAGE SHOULD BE PRESENTED

The integrity of a message is affected by a whole host of things that determine whether it is taken seriously or not:

- *Format*. How is the message put across? Are there visual images that are associated with it? The care taken with the physical presentation of a corporate identity is a good example of this. The appropriate words, even typeface, must be used to get across the impact of the message. Bold, joking messages often use brash, elaborate type-faces, serious material uses serif typefaces. A financial institute is probably not going to use cartoons to put across a death benefit product.

- *Tone*. Choice of language is very important. All messages need to have careful attention paid to the mood, atmosphere or style that they are trying to portray. The mood might be upbeat or sombre. This point is carefully linked to the format issue.
- *Context*. The context in which a message is seen is vital. If, for example, you announce your company results on the day a stock market slide occurs, your performance is bound to be affected too.
- *Timing*. It is no use pumping out information about your special Christmas offers if Christmas was last week.
- *Repetition*. Obviously the more often a credible message is repeated, the more likely it is to be heard and picked up. However, there are instances where familiarity breeds contempt and care has to be taken not to repeat messages for the sake of it or they will become devalued. Using a raft of communication channels can help, since in the mind of the receiver there can be a reinforcement of credibility if they see the message in different contexts and endorsed by different media and other third parties.

Having control over all these factors is likely to be a tall order. We all have horror stories to tell about how our meticulously timed press release was ruined because of a particular item in the news. Equally, there are always opportunities that suddenly occur which we feel we have to take advantage of even if the context is not the best possible.

Sometimes the choice of media in which a message is relayed is restricted. An annual report is a legal document and some of the information in it is strictly regulated. At other times the message imperative will dictate the communication channel. A product recall dictates that advertising will be used to get the message out as quickly and in as controlled a format as possible.

It is often the case that publics and messages are not given the attention they deserve in public relations programmes. Publics tend to be approached as being large uniform blocks, while all the research to date shows that even groupings with the same name have many sub-groups within them, some of which are active, some of which are not.

A careful appreciation of where a public stands is essential for well-founded public relations programmes.

Similarly, general messages are all very well in themselves, but particular audiences should be served by particular messages if the communication is to do a specific job of work. Vague content in communication brings about vague results. Carefully researched, sharply refined and aimed messages with achievable desired effects are what is required.

7

Strategy and tactics

GETTING THE STRATEGY RIGHT

Devising the strategy for a plan or campaign is the most difficult part of the planning process. If the strategy is right, everything else rolls off the back of it.

Rather than thinking of a cohesive and coherent strategy, many practitioners move straight to tactics, the 'What shall we do?' part of the programme, rather than thinking carefully about how the overall programme should be shaped. They then end up with a fragmented, unfocused effort which lacks any underpinning direction or driving force.

Strategy, like planning, applies to total programmes as well as individual activities. It's important because it focuses effort, it gets results and it looks to the long term.

WHAT IS STRATEGY?

Strategy is the overall approach that is taken to a programme or campaign. It is the coordinating theme or factor, the guiding principle, the big idea, the rationale behind the tactical programme.

Strategy is dictated by the issues arising from your analysis of the information at your disposal (see Chapter 4). It is not the same as objectives and it comes before tactics. It is the foundation upon which a tactical programme is built. Strategy is the principle that will move you from where you are now to where you want to be. It is sometimes called 'the big idea'. Sometimes it is: it can be an all-embracing concept. Sometimes it isn't, and you shouldn't be overly concerned if you can't come up with a big idea. You should, however, be very concerned if you don't have a clear rationale.

A very clear if unpleasant example of 'strategy' and 'tactics' was demonstrated in the war conducted by the combined forces which moved against Iraq following that country's invasion of Kuwait (a particularly appropriate example bearing in mind the military origins of the two words):

The objective:	to get the Iraqis out of Kuwait
The strategy:	according to General Colin Powell was to cut them (the Iraqis) off and kill them
The tactics:	pincer movement of ground forces to cut the Iraqis off from Iraq, carpet bombing, divisionary tactics, cutting bridges and so on

Further examples of the relationship between objectives, strategy and tactics are given in Table 7.1.

Table 7.1 *Examples of objectives, strategy and tactics*

	Example one (single-objective, short-term campaign)	Example two (longer-term strategic positioning programme)
Objective	Publicise new product or service	Establish market leader perception
Strategy	Mount media relations campaign	Position as industry voice of authority
Tactics	Press conference Press releases Interviews Competition Advertising etc	Research-based reports Quality literature Media relations Speaker platforms Industry forums Award schemes etc

In a nutshell, strategy is *how* you will achieve an objective and tactics are *what* you will do. For large programmes with several elements, eg community relations, employee relations and customer relations, you will have a strategy for each part of the programme.

FROM STRATEGY TO TACTICS

It goes without saying that tactics should be clearly linked to strategy. When developing a tactical programme all the powers of creativity need to be developed, but there are one or two key factors that should be borne in mind:

● *Use strategy to guide brainstorms*. Strategy should not act as a straitjacket, but it does help to keep you focused on the job in hand.

- *Reject non-strategic activities.* Brainstorms are marvellous and stimulating, and all kinds of exciting and wacky ideas can emerge. However, no matter how good the idea, non-strategic activities should be discarded. Don't throw them away completely, as you might be able to use them in a different programme, but if they don't fit in with the strategic thrust of this programme, they need to be put on one side.
- *Relate tactics to strategy and strategy to objectives.* There should be a definite logical progression. Objectives give the overall direction to the programme – what needs to be achieved. Strategy provides the driving force, the 'how to', and tactics give the general programme in detail, what you will do on a day-to-day basis.
- *Test tactics where possible.* It is always advisable to find out as far as possible if a particular tactic will work. You might know it will work because you've done similar things before, in a slightly different context, but you might be treading in new territory. You need to test its feasibility as far as possible. Thus, if you want to run a series of competitions in the regional press, you had better contact two or three papers to find out if they are in sympathy with the idea.

Here is a point to bear in mind. If you have carefully thought through your strategy and it is the right one to use, you should always change tactics before you change the strategy. A strategic review is a major step. It is likely that you are doing something wrong at the tactical level if a programme is not working as it should.

Of course, planning must build in some flexibility of approach. Sometimes when moving on to the tactics of a campaign it is suddenly realised that a particular tactic, or group of tactics, bears the strategic thrust of the programme. For example, maybe a company has a problem with name recognition (people remember the products but not the organisation). It could well be that new literature is recommended together with a revamp of the Web site and making the company name larger on the products. Putting this into practice may lead the public relations professional to the conclusion that a rethink of the company's corporate identity is required, and this then becomes the strategy, giving coherence, direction and a framework around which to hang the communication programme as a whole.

WHAT TACTICS SHOULD YOU EMPLOY?

It would be easy to think up a series of clever ideas and throw them together into some kind of programme. Too often the techniques themselves become the focus of attention rather than the objective they are meant to achieve.

A programme with a variety of publics and objectives will need a variety of techniques.

One way of looking at public relations programmes is to regard them as 'contact and convince' programmes. First of all you identify and contact the relevant target publics, which entails selecting the publics and choosing a channel of communication through which to contact them. Second, you convince them, through the power of your communications messages, that they should think, believe or act in a certain way.

The set of techniques used in a contact programme must reach a sufficient number of target publics and get the message across to them with enough impact so as to influence them in some way. And this must be done at a reasonable cost. So the public relations practitioner needs to select from a menu of activities of the kind shown on pages 123–24.

Careful choices have to be made about the combination of techniques to be used and the balance between the various activities selected. Each technique has its own strengths and weaknesses. The idea is to select a range of techniques that complement each other and which, when taken as a whole, provide a powerful raft of communication to the target group.

Some examples will illustrate the point. If a company wants to launch a new and highly visual product, such as a new range of expensive cosmetics, it is important that techniques are selected that allow the physical qualities of the product to be demonstrated and where there is some opportunity for some two-way communication. Techniques employed might be exhibitions, sending product samples to journalists, brochures with high-quality photographs and a coupon response that can be followed up by sending samples, a media campaign with product samples attached for consumers, sampling opportunities at retail outlets, and demonstrations at fashion events.

In another situation, say where a company chairperson wants to give detailed financial information to some key investors, the visual and tactile aspects would not be so important, neither is the chairperson talking to a mass audience. In this instance it is important that the message is closely controlled, so a media campaign would not be the best method. The methods chosen might be seminars, production of detailed literature and one-to-one or small group briefings. In these instances, the opportunity for one-to-one interaction to check understanding and support would be critical.

Sometimes the type of campaign clearly dictates the selection of techniques. It would be a brave (or foolish) car manufacturer who did not take its new model to motor shows and allow journalists to test drive it.

Likewise, some techniques are more appropriate to certain types of campaigns. In the consumer area stunts and media attention-grabbing, creative ideas are often a part of the programme, but this is not usually the case in serious lobbying campaigns (although sometimes it is).

So, having brainstormed your ideas for your campaign, how do you finally select from the range of techniques that are open to you? There are two tests to apply:

- *Appropriateness*. Will the technique actually reach the target publics you are aiming for? Will they have the right

MEDIA RELATIONS	INTERNAL COMMUNICATION
Press conference	Videos
Press releases	Briefings
Articles and features	Newsletters
One-to-one briefings	Quality guides
Interviews	Compact disc interactive
Background briefings/materials	E-mail
Photography	Intranet
Video news releases	
Web site	
E-mail	
ADVERTISING (PR LED)	CORPORATE IDENTITY
Corporate	Design
Product	Implementation
DIRECT MAIL (PR LED)	SPONSORSHIP
Annual report	Sport
Brochures/leaflets	Arts
Customer reports	Worthy causes
External newsletters	
General literature	
(Also multimedia material)	
EXHIBITIONS	LOBBYING
Trade and Public	One-to-one briefings
Literature	Background material
Sampling	Videos
Demonstrations	Literature
Multimedia	Group briefings
	Hospitality
	Compact discs
	Audio cassettes
CONFERENCES	RESEARCH
Multimedia	Organisations
Literature	Public relations programmes
Hospitality	Issues monitoring
	Results monitoring
COMMUNITY RELATIONS	CRISIS MANAGEMENT
Direct involvement	Planning
Gifts-in-kind	Implementation
Sponsorship	
Donations	

SPECIAL EVENTS	LIAISON
AGMs	Internal (including counselling)
SGMs	External
Special occasions	
CUSTOMER RELATIONS	**FINANCIAL RELATIONS**
Media relations	Annual report
Direct mail	Briefing materials
Advertising	One-to-one briefing
Internet	Media relations
Exhibitions	Hospitality
Retail outlets	Internet
Sponsorship	Extranet
Product literature	
Newsletters	

amount of impact? Is this a credible and influential technique to carry the message you are waiting to relay? Will the message get through using this technique? Do the techniques suit the message (content, tone, creative treatment)? Is it compatible with other communication devices that the organisation is using?

- *Deliverability.* Can you implement these techniques successfully? Can it be done within the budget and to the required timescale? Do you have the right people with the right expertise to implement the techniques?

Having made the decisions about which broad techniques to employ, consideration has to be given to the specific media to use. Thus, if it is decided that an exhibition is a most suitable technique, we then ask which exhibition needs to be attended? Here judgements have to be made on areas such as how many of your target publics attend the list of available exhibitions. There may be a particular sub-set you need to contact. How does the cost compare between the different exhibitions and which is most cost-effective to you? What sort of fellow exhibitors will there be and are they likely to enhance or detract from your reputation? How influential are those exhibitions? Can you afford not to be there? Who needs who is of importance to you, for example the media? What are the logistical practicalities of you attending one as opposed to another exhibition?

It is in the area of tactics that creativity can shine. A good creative idea adds sparkle and difference to a campaign, and it doesn't have to be entirely wacky either. A nice example is provided by a residential care community looking after mentally handicapped adults. The members of the community are virtually self-sufficient and a key part of their working lives centres on a farm. To encourage support, the community sends out packs of postcards, showing, in high-quality photographs, the life and surroundings of community members. It is a simple and effective way for the community to encourage others to support their work.

DIFFERENT CAMPAIGNS NEED DIFFERENT TACTICS

To illustrate different approaches using very different techniques, here are three detailed case studies. All the campaigns have been successful – they won IPR Excellence Awards – but they were aimed at very different audiences and therefore required quite different treatments.

'A Night At The Opera' conducted by Shandwick International on behalf of Harry Ramsden's fish and chip restaurant in Edinburgh, Scotland

Fish and chips and opera? A strange combination or a natural mix?

Harry Ramsden's fish and chip restaurant in Edinburgh is a franchise operation, seating 170 people in comfort and style, and caters primarily for families and for the slightly older generation. Traditionally during the autumn and winter months the number of diners at Harry's falls dramatically (averaging between 10 and 20 diners a night) compared to the spring and summer months (when it can average between 90 and 130). To counteract this fall in diners and the subsequent fall in income, Shandwick International suggested that a programme of monthly events, held during this quiet time of the year, could help attract diners and help reduce the decline. Monday nights were chosen for the special events, as these were seen as being the 'quietest'.

Client objectives

The client had two objectives:

- to attract more customers to the restaurant during the winter months;
- to make a clear net profit from any promotional activity.

Target audience

The target audience was the general public and OAPs within the central belt of Scotland, living within a 30–40 mile radius of Edinburgh.

Strategy

The strategy was to create a series of 'unique' and memorable dining experiences never before seen in Scotland during the months of September to February that would each attract at least 100 people to the restaurant.

Planning

Shandwick International contacted Scottish Opera to propose a series of performances in the Edinburgh restaurant on the last Monday of the month, starting in September 1998 and running through to February 1999. Scottish Opera was targeted because the consultancy had read recent newspaper reports stating its wish to take opera 'out of the theatre' and 'to the masses'. Scottish Opera agreed immediately to the proposal.

A timetable of opera nights was placed firmly in the diary, and Shandwick International produced a critical time path of promotional activity to maximise attendance. A price of £16.50 per person was agreed, which if 100 people dined would cover entertainment, staff and food costs, and would net the owners a small profit of £400. It was thought that the first opera night would make a loss, but that other opera nights would make up for this.

Action

The key tactics employed were:

- Shandwick International produced leaflets and posters that were displayed in the restaurant to attract regular diners. Owing to the slightly older nature of some of the customers, leaflets and posters were also distributed to churches, golf clubs, bowling clubs, social clubs and charity shops in Edinburgh.
- Flyers were posted to the database of customers held on file at the restaurant. Scottish Opera gave Shandwick International access to a database of its patrons, who were invited to attend the opening night.
- A media relations programme was implemented, commencing with a press release about the first 'Scottish Opera Night at Harry Ramsden's'. Broadcast and press media response to the unusual concept of 'Opera & Chips', was significant.
- This was followed up by one-to-one phone calls to relevant journalists. Down-the-line media interviews were held with the owners of Harry Ramsden's as well as with key spokespeople within Scottish Opera.
- Shandwick International then issued a photocall, inviting a broad range of targeted media to attend the opening opera night. The list of media included news and picture-desk editors from broadcast and print media, and food and music critics. Media coverage was obtained prior to and after the opera night.

Measurement

The campaign significantly overachieved its objectives:

- On each of the opera nights, over 165 people dined.
- There was a waiting list of 20–30 people at each event ready to take the place of anyone who didn't turn up.
- On three nights, just under 200 people attended.
- In total, just over 1,000 diners attended the opera nights, netting Harry Ramsden's over £9,750 in profit.
- Many diners booked again for further opera nights and have dined at Harry Ramsden's on other occasions.
- Comment cards placed in the restaurant and filled in by diners stated that they had booked after reading articles in the press.
- Media coverage was obtained as follows:
  - Broadcast:
    STV News, BBC Radio 4: 'The Food Programme', BBC Radio Scotland's breakfast programme, Radio Forth and Scot FM;
  - Press:
    The Times, Daily Express, The Sun, The Daily Record, Daily Mail, The Independent on Sunday, The Scotsman Weekend Magazine (two insertions), *Scotland on Sunday* and *Edinburgh Evening News*.

Budget

The budget for the campaign was £5,000.

Points about the campaign

There are some key points to draw out about the campaign, concerning strategy and tactics:

- The strategy was clearly linked to the objectives of the campaign.
- A tight budget doesn't necessarily mean an unambitious campaign! It can be a spur to creativity. In this case

Shandwick International put Scottish Opera's objective of getting out into the community together with their public relations task and came up with a partnership that suited both organisations at minimal cost.

- If you don't think big or 'outside the box', you may miss great opportunities. Who would have thought of putting opera and chips together?!
- The raft of tactics – press, flyers, targeted mailings, posters – reinforced and complemented each other.
- The media angle was spot on: quirky, new, photogenic and fun.
- Behind the campaign was careful planning and meticulous implementation.

'Power to the Pre-Schools' conducted by Fishburn Hedges and Wallace Connections on behalf of the Pre-School Learning Alliance

Community-based, parent-run pre-schools have existed for more than 35 years, cater for 850,000 children and are thus the major form of provision for children under five. Operating outside the maintained school system, they received virtually no public funding and insufficient recognition.

Nursery vouchers, introduced by John Major's Conservative government, provided resources for pre-schools but turned out to be a disastrous experiment. The Pre-School Learning Alliance welcomed the additional funding represented by nursery vouchers, but opposed the mechanism on the grounds that it would generate excessive competition. It was right. Local Education Authorities took the opportunity of vouchers to admit four-year-olds into primary schools to create a new income stream. Reception classes were not and are not regulated in the same way as other forms of nursery provision and so can and often do have more than 30 four-year-olds with only one classroom teacher. This practice of warehousing four-year-olds in maintained schools led directly to the closure in 1997 of 800 pre- schools and the prediction that a further 1,500 would close in 1998.

On its election, the Labour government was sceptical about the value of pre-schools and some Labour politicians resented the charity's independent stance over vouchers. In addition, teaching unions and many Labour-controlled local authorities held longstanding beliefs that nursery education should be provided by maintained schools.

The Pre-School Learning Alliance, its PR consultancy, Wallace Connections, and its public affairs agency, Fishburn Hedges, worked together to plan and deliver the 'Pre-Schools Matter' campaign which culminated in a day of celebration and campaigning on 6 May 1998.

Client objectives

The client had two objectives:

- to half the closure of pre-schools;
- to demonstrate that pre-schools could play a part in delivering the government's educational promises.

Strategy

The strategic elements of the campaign were that:

- it should have a local as well as a national focus;
- it should draw on the commitment and energy of the charity's 40,000 volunteers, 100,000 pre-school staff and the million parents who use pre-schools;
- it should build on the warm relations that already existed between the media and the charity;
- it should extend parliamentary and political contacts; and
- rather than be concerned solely with complaining about closures, it should have a positive and celebratory feeling, reflecting the creative and playful side of the charity's work, as well as its more serious purpose.

Messages

The following messages to the government and to local authorities were identified:

- Pre-schools offer a cost-effective means of helping to deliver a whole range of Labour's manifesto commitments and are an example of the so-called 'third way' in action.
- Pre-schools are a cost-effective means of delivering nursery education, but offer added value through the involvement of parents in terms of lifelong learning, family learning, support for lone parents, combating social exclusion and the provision of gateways from welfare into work.
- Pre-school closures undermine the government's capacity to deliver across these fronts. Not only can the new government not do without pre-schools but with the necessary support, pre-schools could do much more.

Planning

The team agreed that it had to win round New Labour to the view that pre-schools should be central to delivering its agenda on extending nursery education, developing childcare, tackling social exclusion, raising school standards, implementing the New Deal and promoting widened access to lifelong learning. Central to this was the need to persuade the government to take urgent action to stop the closure of pre-schools and to set out a framework for the future that would allow pre-schools to play a growing part in early years' education and childcare. A campaign was planned using a combination of high-profile media and public relations as well as contact building and lobbying to maximise its impact.

Action

Key tactics leading up to 6 May 1998 included:

- the launch of the campaign to the charity's own membership in 1997;
- a series of meetings and briefings for key print and broadcast journalists;
- a programme of meetings with ministers, special advisers and officials from the Department for Education and Employment (DfEE), HM Treasury, the Department of Social Security, the Department of Health, the Number 10 Policy Unit, the Social Exclusion Unit and the Home Office;
- a formal launch of the campaign in February 1998 with MPs and celebrities;
- a package of materials for the charity's 20,000 pre-schools which included petition forms, posters and special briefing materials;
- a campaign lapel pin;
- regular and frequent briefings to key charity activists;
- a meeting for sympathetic MPs in the House of Commons, as a result of which an Early Day Motion attracted 72 signatures;
- a message of support from each of the three main party leaders;
- local briefings and visits to pre-schools for MPs;
- swift reaction in late March 1998 to a government announcement that all four-year-olds would have a nursery place – ensuring widespread coverage of the issue and the shortcomings of reception classes for four-year-olds.

Huge exercise

The main campaign day on 6 May 1998 was a huge exercise in event management. Hundreds of pre-school leaders from up and down the country came to London. David Blunkett, the education secretary, addressed a specially-arranged conference alongside celebrities and leading figures from education, the church and journalism. All those attending the conference went in procession across Blackfriars Bridge (while London's only fireboat carried out a special 20-minute display with its fire hoses), accompanied by a double-decker bus laden with the signed petition forms, to join a massive family fun day on the South Bank.

Later that day, following a balloon release, the petition with more than 150,000 signatures was delivered by charity principals, celebrities, parents and children – who travelled to Westminster on the customised double-decker bus – to an all-party group of MPs. More than 100 individual pre-school leaders lobbied their MPs and the day was rounded off with a reception in the Commons attended by ministers, shadow ministers, peers and MPs. In addition, more than 90 local events were organised at branch level by the charity.

On the morning of 6 May, pre-school children delivered a birthday cake and card to Number 10 – it was the prime minister's 46th birthday. Number 10 had been briefed beforehand and, to the delight (and surprise) of all those involved, Tony Blair opened the door and welcomed the children in front of the cameras. The front page of the *Evening Standard*, all of the TV news bulletins and *The Independent* and the *Daily Express* carried pictures of the event. A question about pre-schools was asked at Prime Minister's Question Time.

Measurement

Number 10 and David Blunkett had been briefed that a gesture of support was required to show the pre-school movement that the government appreciated its work.

- David Blunkett announced in his speech to the conference that the government was setting up a fund of £500,000 of new money specifically to stem the tide of pre-school closures. He also announced that pre-schools would be able to benefit from a £6 million fund to boost 'wrap around' childcare.

- Mr Blunkett stated the government's unequivocal support for the pre-school movement and specifically mentioned the important role pre-schools should play in Labour's policies on expanding nursery provision for three-year-olds, in childcare, and in combating social exclusion. He added: 'We do not want rising fours in receptions classes.'

- Tony Blair wrote in his letter of support for the campaign: 'The Pre-School Learning Alliance is right: pre-schools do matter … They have much to contribute to our policies on family learning, childcare and social exclusion … I share your concern that many good pre-schools are closing or face closure, and we are discussing with your chief executive how we can help to prevent that.'

- Coverage of the day was achieved from Radio 4's 'Today' programme to the major BBC, ITN, Channel Four, Sky and other TV news bulletins, to Radio 5 Live, Radio 1 and IRN, and to coverage in the national and regional press the following day.

- The effects of the campaign have continued well beyond its initial time frame. Since May 1998, further responses to Parliament by David Blunkett have directly referred to the advice of the Pre-school Learning Alliance, and DfEE guidelines on early years education aimed at local authorities have been significantly amended – for example, they now require local authorities to involve bodies such as the Pre-School Learning Alliance in their decision-making procedures.

Conclusion

Ever since autumn 1996, when pre-school closures caused by nursery vouchers were first brought to light, the Pre-school Learning Alliance has been campaigning actively for action to stop them. The 'Pre-Schools Matter' campaign finally succeeded in persuading the new government of the need for action. Much more will need to be done to guarantee the future of pre-schools, but the campaign has started the process.

Points about the campaign

From this campaign there are again a number of learning points about strategy and tactics:

- The campaign was complex, so one strategy was inappropriate. A number of elements had to be woven together to ensure success.
- The campaign took the unusual tack of focusing on celebration rather than just pleading a cause – a different psychological approach.
- Message content and successful delivery are absolutely critical.
- Although the campaign involved an enormous number of people and there were potentially a large number of tactics and stunts that could have been organised at the national level, it kept its focus on a small number of high-impact events so that effort would not be dissipated. Local groups were given free reign, because those on the ground know their local audiences.
- The involvement of key opinion formers and decision-makers was critical: once they were persuaded, the rest, as they say, was easy.

'Attrition by Charm' in-house campaign by the 8th (Co Armagh and Co Tyrone) Battalion of the Royal Irish Regiment

The 8th (Co Armagh and Co Tyrone) Battalion is one of six Home Service Battalions of the Royal Irish Regiment. The battalion is over 700 strong and has been continuously deployed on counter-terrorist operations in Armagh and Tyrone, Northern Ireland, for over 20 years. Eighty-seven members of the battalion have been killed by terrorists on and off duty and the battalion cares for over 170 bereaved relatives and disabled soldiers. Unlike General Service units, soldiers in the Royal Irish Regiment Home Service live out of barracks, in the community. This places them in a unique position involving some danger. It also gives them immense local knowledge and continuity of service.

Against the backcloth of political change in 1998, the 8th Battalion, based in the divided city of Armagh, with its geographic, religious and political significance, has faced a most challenging operational environment. While much of the Province enjoyed, to an extent, the benefits of declared ceasefires and minimal military patrolling, the Armagh Police subdivision experienced more serious terrorist incidents and examples of sectarian violence than any other. The presence of the military on the ground had not reduced, being essential to the Royal Ulster Constabulary (RUC), providing unquantifiable reassurance to the whole community, and demanding stamina and a most professional approach from all ranks.

The Royal Irish Regiment Home Service, because of personal security concerns and its direct operational role in support of the RUC, has traditionally found it very difficult to publicise its impartiality and support to the community. This case study illustrates how the 8th Royal Irish has overcome these obstacles in its bid to facilitate a solution in Northern Ireland and been seen as part of the solution, not the problem.

Objective

To become part of the solution for peace in Northern Ireland.

Internal action

The first significant steps in demonstrating that the 8th Royal Irish, a local batallion, was capable of identifying with *all* communities, with an impartial knowledge and understanding of different traditions, were taken in late 1997. The battalion invested heavily in a series of ethical study evenings for all soldiers. These were linked to visits and workshops that explored everything from the Orange Order and Gaelic Games to peace and reconciliation groups. This inward investment included the formation of an Irish language evening class. Run weekly by a local Christian Brother, the class, attended by Protestant and Catholic soldiers of all ranks, has done much to improve knowledge of Gaelic culture. A bid has now been made to recognise this achievement by offering an Army colloquial language qualification to the students.

Planning

Concurrently with internal marketing and education of the 'workforce', a corporate public relations/community relations plan was formulated and for the first time ever published as part of the commanding officer's annual directive. At last, public relations was a weapon in the arsenal of peace and 'Attrition by Charm' was launched. The battalion researched local and national media outlets in both communities that would report achievements in a genuine, positive and balanced manner. The support of local opinion formers was sought and involved in as many projects as possible, as an interest was taken in community priorities. This was a major undertaking, leading to many visits to the battalion. A battalion presentation team was formed to take their message into the wider community, so that they would be regarded as *'part of the solution, not the problem'*.

Having published the battalion plan and conducted briefings and rehearsals, everything was ready for action – except that there was no budget! During planning, costings for everything from photographic support to transport and event management had been undertaken. Understanding that no specific budget would be allocated, the battalion realised that it would have to keep the plan flexible, so that costs could be absorbed into existing budgets for training, recruiting and administration. This was easily achievable as every public relations objective set had spin-offs for each of these areas.

For specific public events, such as the 'Last Night of the Pom Poms' (involving Chris De Burgh, Riverdance, the Royal Opera and the regimental band), the battalion set about raising corporate and individual sponsorship (thus involving the community even further), to cover costs and to allow it to raise considerable sums for local charities.

Action

Building on this foundation, in 1998 the battalion hosted some ground-breaking cross-community events. It brought together 300 school-children from across the Province and the Republic of Ireland for a series of adventure weekends, known as 'Ex Action Ranger', and through a similar event called 'Ex Mission Impossible', it brought together groups of adults from all walks of life and traditions to experience Army life for a weekend, while at the same time raising money through sponsorship for a cross-community charity. These events, at which doctors from Belfast rubbed shoulders with plumbers from Derry or even Dublin, not only broke down inter-community barriers but also changed long-held views of the regiment and possibly the Army. They also made ideal human-interest stories which built on the peace process.

Through sport and music the battalion demonstrated the range of talents it possessed, and its openness. Also in 1998 the Battalion Half Marathon (until then a closed military event) was moved into the local area and opened to all runners from all communities, thereby attracting publicity from the sports media. Local pipers and other traditional musicians and dancers joined forces with the military band for musical workshops and events. A battalion boxing competition featured boxers from civilian boxing clubs as well as novices from within the battalion for the first time. Links with the community were further enhanced through the sharing of regimental traditions, such as the wearing of shamrock on St Patrick's Day, opening the base and surrounding area to allow people to watch a spectacular fireworks display run at

Halloween, and hosting the Armagh District Scout AGM. Many of these embryonic events had to be handled extremely carefully, with no publicity, as both sides built confidence and trust in each other.

Measurement

These cross-community events, together with a number of other set-piece charity fundraisers and visits, coupled with a much increased media profile, have exposed the regiment to large numbers of people who had never had an opportunity to discover for themselves what the soldiers were like. In one year alone the batallion raised over £30,000 for good causes in the Province, while strengthening links with every part of the local community and earning the respect and support of many. The battalion also achieved over 100 positive mentions in local, regional and national media (97 more than the previous year!) and all done at little or no cost.

Points about the campaign

- You don't have to spend lots of money to undertake a successful programme.
- Cross-linking to other organisations' activities (eg training, regimental band concerts) meant that the public relations campaign piggy-backed their budgets!
- Time, care and attention to detail is all important.
- Nothing tests your sincerity more than living the public relations message in the community.
- Don't underestimate the value of sponsorship or the willingness of sponsors to cooperate if they see the cause is worthwhile.

SUSTAINING LONG-TERM PROGRAMMES

One of the key issues in longer-term public relations programmes is sustainability. How do you keep a programme going year after year and maintain focus and interest?

Running a campaign with a single, short-term objective that is achieved in a determined timescale, eg holding a Christmas party for employees and their families, is rather different from sustaining a long-running programme on financial advice.

Here is an example of a long-running programme that has 'rolled-out' over many years.

Lansons Communications campaign for IFA Promotion Limited, the organisation representing Britain's independent financial advisers

In 1993 Lansons Communications began a new approach to IFA Promotion's marketing strategy. A year-long campaign called 'Tax Action' focused on the £8 billion paid every year in unnecessary tax. The solution was for people to use Independent Financial Advisors (IFAs) to get the correct professional financial advice. IFA Promotion ran a consumer hotline which gave callers the names and addresses of their three nearest IFAs. The campaign was a great success and responses to the hotline increased by 160 per cent.

The task in 1994 was to build upon the success of the previous year, to convince more ABC1s to use professional advisers and to contact the hotline. Promoting independent financial advice as the preferred route and convincing IFAs to run marketing initiatives based on IFA Promotion's lead was an ongoing objective.

The new campaign was designed to keep the best of 'Tax Action' and to broaden its appeal. It also aimed to add to the theme. 'Britain's Undiscovered Billions' looked at all the money wasted each year through financial mismanagement or inertia. Two new types of waste apart from tax were highlighted: 'dead money', the focus being missed return because money not needed day to day is left idle (often in current accounts); and 'buried treasure', money that is rightfully ours but left unclaimed, eg from legacies, premium bonds and state benefits.

The underpinning of Undiscovered Billions was research done by Mintel that quantified the waste. This research was based on an analysis of the Inland Revenue's own 'Personal Income Survey', which gives an in-depth analysis of 70,000 individual cases. Additional data were obtained from the Target Group Index survey conducted by BMRB International (British Market Research Bureau) among 25,000 adults each year, and other conclusions were based on industry analysis. The research discovered that in 1994 British people could have been £12 billion better off – an average of £300 per adult – if only they had managed their finances better.

Lansons used the research as a platform both for a national and media campaign and a local marketing campaign run by IFAs. Following the launch, the Mintel figures were used to launch 12 separate public relations initiatives. These mini-campaigns, rolled out at a rate of two per month, covered topics such as holiday currency and money wasted by not shopping around for insurance.

Lansons also put together a 'case studies' database of people helped by IFAs for use by the press (150 IFAs country-wide cooperated). Video news release footage based on real-life case studies was also prepared and an advertorial campaign, run with the Newspaper Society, was taken up by over 100 regional newspapers. The IFAs themselves came to training seminars, where they were given guidance on using a marketing pack containing adverts, draft client letters, posters, case studies, a summary of the Mintel finding, and a copy of the *Money Detector* booklet that was given out free when people contacted the hotline.

The results of the 1994/95 campaign were exceptional. In the first five months of the campaign, 46,500 people contacted the IFA Promotion hotline, up by 58 per cent from 1993, and over 40,000 people requested the *Money Detector* booklet.

IFA Promotion's annual Gallup monitoring survey showed that 56 per cent of ABC1 adults were likely to go to IFAs for advice. Recognition of the blue IFA logo went up from 41 to 52 per cent. Over 75 per cent of IFA Promotion's 4,000-strong membership took part in the 'Tax Action' campaign.

Every national newspaper bar one covered the campaign in its first two weeks. The BBC made a programme called 'Here and Now' based on the issues, using IFA Promotion material. The theme they developed was 'Taxbusters'. The findings were also featured in the BBC's 'Good Fortunes' programme. The IFA Promotion's chief executive was interviewed by 30 radio stations.

So, how can the momentum of such a successful programme be maintained over subsequent years?

The 'Tax Action' theme has provided the backbone of Lansons work for IFA Promotion and has ensured a constant level of media coverage. Tax is a recurring theme in the lives of every adult each year and Lansons are able to capitalise on this, publishing the findings of IFA Promotion's 'Tax Action' investigation annually. The results are regionalised to give local as well as national media appeal. For example, the 1998 investigation revealed that nearly two million people in Wales (that's three out of four Welsh tax payers) unnecessarily paid a total of £340 million, either through inertia or because of lack of understanding of the taxation rules.

Having a long-term theme does not mean that the programme is simply an updating process. According to Lansons, the opportunity is now taken to capitalise on the financial issues of the moment and those that they can predict. So in 1999, apart from the regular 'Tax Action' investigation, they pushed the fact that this was the last year in which PEPs and TESSAs could be taken out and the first in which the new ISAs could be opened. The advice of an IFA was needed to ensure wise investment.

The public relations campaign has also been extended to include coverage of IFA Promotion on the Internet. Consumers who read about IFAs can click on a link to the IFA Promotion Web site, where they can 'Find an IFA'.

The Millennium was too good an opportunity to miss!

BMRB International was commissioned to find out how adults in the UK wanted to change their lives in the new dawn. The research revealed that nearly 20 per cent wanted to change their homes, 16 per cent their jobs, 14 per cent their love lives, over 11 per cent their careers and over 21 per cent their health and fitness. For 14 per cent (6.5 million people), lack of money was the hindering factor in making their desired changes.

By focusing not only on finance but on other things such as love life and careers, Lansons had numerous hooks for the news and general-interest media, as well as for the personal finance journalists. This approach also formed the basis of a Web-based fun-but-serious 'personality test', which provided initial information on finance but pointed the way to the IFAs.

Points about this campaign

- Identifying a thorny issue (tax) that is a feature of every working adult's life and which has an annual focus (the tax return) ensures a built-in interest..
- Because people are interested in the issue, so are the media.
- Making material as pertinent as possible to individuals is vitally important; use of the regional media is a major tactic.
- Use of the Internet facilitates response to individual information requests.
- Capitalising on issues of the moment – and of tomorrow – keeps the role of the IFAs to the front of people's minds throughout the year, not just when the tax return is done. It also helps to set the media agenda by indicating those issues that will be of interest in the near future.
- The role of public relations is to generate awareness and interest, not to sell individual products, which is a job best left to the regulated experts.

THE BIG 'WHAT IF?' – CONTINGENCY PLANNING

All good public relations plans cater for the unexpected. There isn't room in this book to go into the whole area of crisis management. That subject, along with issues management, is dealt with in *Risk Issues and Crisis Management in Public Relations*, another book in this series.

However, it is necessary to be prepared for the unexpected at both the strategic and tactical levels. At the strategic level we need a contingency plan in place for one of three possibilities:

- if the reputation of the organisation is damaged;
- if its financial position is jeopardised;
- if its trading operation is interrupted.

These are major crises requiring an immediate response that needs planning. Examples of activities that might precipitate such a crisis are new or proposed legislation, product withdrawal, an acquisition or takeover, strikes, an act of terrorism, a factory closure or heavy redundancies.

In some of these situations tightening up on quality control, improving industrial relations or improving the quality of your intelligence-gathering processes could help prevent problems becoming crises. It is the public relations professional's job to look out for the possible problem areas and to ensure that there are plans in place to deal with the communication implications. It will be necessary to liaise with other key people in the organisation such as the chief executive, marketing function, sales/distribution, finance and quality areas, not to mention the lawyers and insurance advisers.

As the public relations professional your tasks will probably include:

- planning for potential crises with others in the company;
- helping to put together a crisis management team and ensuring there is clear communication between members;
- helping to put together the crisis plan;
- initiating 'trial-runs' of the plan;
- keeping the plan up to date;
- training key members of staff to handle the media;
- ensuring media enquiries are planned for;
- putting together key policy statements;
- acting as a part of the crisis management team if required;
- monitoring the results of crises to improve contingency plans.

Of course, at the strategic level, each of the various scenarios will need to be considered in its own right and a separate plan of action developed. There will be common areas in each plan, such as the process for dealing with media, but tailor-made solutions are required for events of such importance.

At the tactical level contingency planning is very much common sense. This requires a careful examination of each tactic in the programme to find out what might go wrong. Thus, if an outdoor event is planned, what happens if the weather is bad? What if there are accidents or incidents at the event? What if some of the equipment fails? A balance has to be struck between the ideal and the realistic. If you have arranged a fireworks show you don't have another display ready just in case, but you do ensure that as much checking is done as possible, and you might ensure that one part of the display is kept in reserve and used at the end if all goes to plan. You'll certainly ensure that there are umbrellas available or a covered stand so that people are kept dry.

Planning the strategy and tactics of a campaign is fun. It is challenging and demanding, both intellectually and creatively, but there is something uniquely rewarding about planning and then executing a programme that is well thought out and well judged. Good public relations plans don't just come from the blue, they are the result of much hard work and consideration. To come up with a strategy that works requires a great deal of research and incisive thinking to get to the heart of the matter. Tactics, too, should be chosen not just because they are imaginative, but also because they are appropriate to the publics towards whom they are directed and because they are without doubt the correct medium to carry the message.

Planning with care puts the practitioner in control. It enhances the probability of success and it ensures that the right things are focused on.

8

Timescales and resources

TIMESCALES

Two things are certain in a public relations practitioner's life. The first is that there is never enough time to do everything that needs to be done – the tasks and possibilities for action are always far greater than the time available. The second is that because public relations tasks often involve other people and the co-ordination of several elements, it always takes longer than you think to get the job done.

There are two interlinked key factors that must be observed when considering timescales. The first is that deadlines must be identified so that the tasks associated with a project can be completed on time. The second is that the right resources need to be allocated so that the tasks in hand can be completed.

Deadlines can be internally or externally imposed. Examples of internally imposed deadlines might be company keynote events such as the announcement of the chief executive's retirement; the announcement of an acquisition; the diaries of the people who might be involved in the public relations programme.

Externally imposed deadlines might be that you have to be involved in fixed events such a major shows and exhibitions like the Boat Show or the Badminton Horse Trials. There might be calendar dates that have to be worked to like Christmas or Valentine's Day. Then there may be what would be regarded as most appropriate dates. Ideally you would launch your new garden products in the spring when most people start to work in their gardens, but technically you could launch them at any time.

So how do you ensure that deadlines are met? The key thing is to identify all the individual tasks that have to be done in order for a project to be completed. Below is a list of the main elements of a straightforward press conference:

- Draw up invitation list.
- Organise venue.
- Book catering.
- Issue invitations.
- Book multimedia equipment.
- Write speeches.
- Prepare presentation materials.
- Prepare media packs.
- Follow up invitations.
- Prepare final attendance list.
- Rehearsals.
- Attend conference.
- Follow up.

Each of these elements then needs breaking down further into all the component parts. Thus, for example, a fairly simple press pack might have in it a press release, some background briefing material, photographs, some product literature or a brochure and a specially designed press folder. To put the pack together will include briefing and monitoring designers, printers and photographers, writing the press material, liaising with the marketing department to get the product literature, liaising with senior management to get approval for the material, reproducing the press release and background briefing, collating the press packs and organising delivery to the conference.

CRITICAL PATH ANALYSIS

Having split the project into its individual components, timings have to be attached. A useful technique here is critical path analysis (CPA) which identifies those elements of a programme that involve the greatest amount of time. It is these elements that dictate when a project can be completed. CPA also recognises that more than one task can be undertaken at a time and therefore enables you to work as efficiently as possible. Thus, a critical path for our press packs may be as shown in Figure 8.1 on page 151.

This represents a very tight timetable, and assumes that designers, printers and photographers are all available. Sometimes, of course, they are not. In practice most professionals will have a number of suppliers they can call on, and most projects do not begin from a standing start as shown in the example. However, the principle holds. Several things have to be done to put together a simple press pack, and they need to be carefully co-ordinated and timed with, preferably, a little contingency at the end (notice a whole day for collation and another one for delivery, with an intervening weekend) in case of emergencies. It is also good practice to get as much done as early as possible to give time at the end for any unforeseen problems. It would have been possible to brief the photographer on Day 4 and still have the prints back in time to collate the packs, but it would have been pushing things.

Obviously, if you are pushed for time and need to complete the task earlier, ways must be sought to shorten some of the critical path activities. It may be, for example, that you decide to use an existing company folder to put your press material in. Or it may be by allocating additional resources and paying the designer to work the weekend, you can produce a folder in a shortened timescale.

If by shortening the crucial path as much as possible a fixed deadline cannot be met, the activity itself must be questioned and an alternative communication technique selected.

To go back to the use of the critical path, having once broken down the putting together of the press packs into its own critical path, this can then be put into the larger critical path for the press conference as a whole.

The final programme might look something like that shown in Figure 8.2 on page 153.

There are several project planning software programs now on the market that will produce automatic schedules and diary prompts, but you still have to do the basic groundwork of deciding how long a task will take and who is involved, so knowing about CPA is important.

Like any other person, it is important that public relations practitioners manage their time effectively, and work as efficiently as possible by having in place practices and procedures that regularise standard tasks, and by planning ahead. Another book in this series, *Public Relations: Practical Guide to the Basics* by Philip Henslowe, gives a whole host of checklists for typical public relations tasks such as event planning and specifications for suppliers. Checklists are the practitioner's friend and should be used to ensure that everything is done that needs to be done.

LONGER-TERM PLANS

Putting together plans for individual projects is all very well, but if care is not taken the big picture is lost. It is absolutely

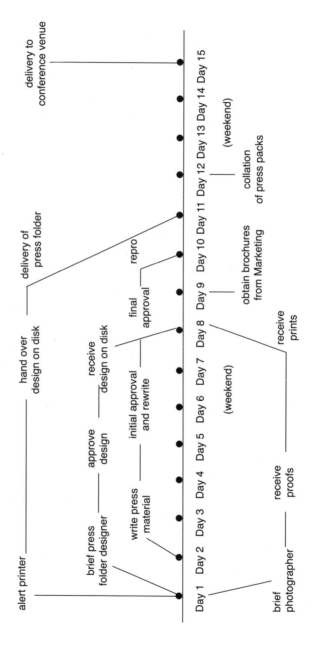

Figure 8.1 *Critical path for putting together a press pack*

essential that the whole campaign or programme is planned in as much detail as possible and an overall timetable for action is constructed. Many practitioners are working to long-term objectives and may have outline plans for a number of years ahead. Getting those plans on paper and approved is important because it helps maintain a focus beyond the immediate here and now. It is very easy to become so embroiled in day-to-day matters that the strategic vision becomes obscured and overall objectives lost.

Certainly, working to at least an annual plan is important. It helps to ensure that things happen when they are supposed to and it gives you control. If other activities arise, you can make a judgement as to whether they or the planned activity should be pursued.

Overleaf is an example of an annual media campaign for a garden centre chain – see Table 8.1 on page 154. It is immediately apparent from it where the peaks of activity are. February, May and August are going to be heavy months, and it might be that extra resources are needed in the form of consultancy or freelance help.

Obviously, a large department or a consultancy carrying out comprehensive programmes will have several activity plans like this covering the whole gamut of public relations work. For example, they could well have an internal communications plan, a community relations plan, a business-to-business plan and so on which will all need to be collated into a prioritised master plan. It is then that decisions on resources will be made. Either the plan will be accepted and resourced accordingly or, as is often the case, resources will be limited and therefore activities will have to be cut from the bottom of the priority list upwards. When making decisions on which areas are to be cut, great care has to be taken to ensure that overall integrity is maintained and that what remains is a well-integrated programme that provides a good complementary raft of activities which address all the essential audiences.

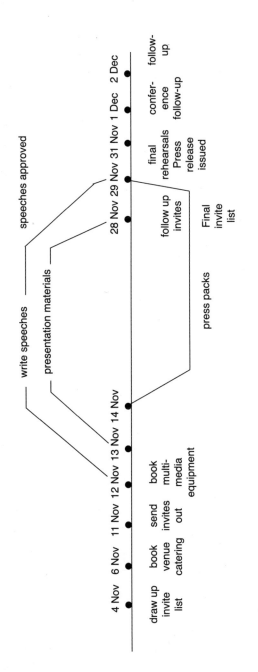

Figure 8.2 *Critical path for press conference*

ACTIVITY	JAN	FEB	MAR	APR	MAY	JUN	JUL	AUG	SEP	OCT	NOV	DEC
EDITOR BRIEFINGS (one-to-one)	Trade press × 2 briefings	Consumer press × 2 briefings	Trade press × 2 briefings	Consumer press × 2 briefings	Trade press × 2 briefings							
Advertorials with key journals (to be negotiated)		*House & Garden*		*Horticultural Journal*		*Garden Answers*		*Horticultural Week*		*Amateur Gardener*		*Royal Horticultural Society Journal*
NEWS STORIES (including new products)	News story	Launch of lawncare advice service	New Centre opening	Launch of tree surgeon service	News story	New Centre opening	Barbecue promotion	News story	New Centre opening	Launch of new power tool range	Christmas plants promotion	New Centre opening
SEASONAL THEMES (for regional press)	Tools		Spring is here		Care of fruit trees and bushes		Pest control		Care of borders		Winter lawncare	
Competitions with local press		Power tools promotion			Garden furniture promotion			Water features promotion			Indoor garden promotion	
Exhibitions					Chelsea Flower Show	Gardeners' World		Royal Horticultural Society				

Table 8.1 *Annual planner for garden centre media campaign*

RESOURCES

Resourcing of public relations programmes comes under three headings. The first is human resources, the second is operating costs and the third is equipment.

Human resources

Whether working in-house or in consultancy the time and skills of individuals have to be paid for. The more experienced and adept the individual, the more expensive he or she is. Clearly the level of human resourcing depends on two things: the size of the programme that is to be undertaken and the nature of the programme.

There are tasks that most competent public relations practitioners would be expected to perform. For example, most would be expected to be able to run a media relations programme and produce literature of a good standard. However, highly complex lobbying programmes demand rarer skills and for that you will pay a premium.

A public relations professional with adequate support can run a reasonably broad-based programme of limited depth. Alternatively he or she can handle a highly focused in-depth programme. The more comprehensive and multi-layered the programme, the more human resources will be required to run it, and the greater the levels of skill and experience needed.

In an ideal world an optimum programme is devised and justified, and the human resources required allocated. More realistically there is a trade-off between the ideal and the human resource overheads that an organisation is prepared to carry.

However, a real problem comes when human resources are cut. Public relations is a relationship-driven activity and relationships are created by people. By cutting human resources the ability of public relations to do its job is severely threatened. When times are tight, every other avenue for cost cutting must be explored before cutting people. This is a battle that is sometimes hard to win because it is usually the human resource costs that are the greatest in a public relations department. A simple comparison with advertising illustrates the point. An advertising department may have a staff bill of £100,000, but spend £1,000,000 on media. If cuts come their way, it could be possible to cut the media bills by, say, £100,000 without causing irreparable harm. The public relations department may also have a staff bill of £100,000, but its operating costs could be very low because the programme focuses on media relations, Internet-based activities and internal communications. Costs might be £50,000 or less.

Costs might be saved by trimming the operating budget by the same percentage as the advertising/media cost budget, but 10 per cent of £50,000 is just £5,000. The obvious 'solution' is to cut the human resources where substantial savings can be made. This could spell disaster. Journalists' reasonable expectations might not be met, Internet publics may be ignored and the internal communications programme may be reduced. Overall the reputation of the organisation will suffer and it may take years to recover.

Operating costs

When costing out public relations activities two key things need to be borne in mind: effectiveness and efficiency.

The right techniques need to be selected in order for a programme to be effective. When the techniques have been chosen it is then incumbent on the good public relations professional to be as efficient as possible. So, for example, it might be decided that an effective way to communicate with important customers is via a magazine. Then choices have to be made on such things as format, number of pages, weight of paper and colour content. There is no need to produce a full-colour magazine just because it looks good. If the message content and the right tone can be set by producing a two-colour magazine, then that should be the choice. Against that position, you might argue that competitors send out colour material and that you can't afford to look cheap by comparison. Similarly, if the publication is to be mailed out, the weight of paper will be critical since that, combined with the number of pages, will determine postage costs. Efficient use of resources is important not only from a management point of view, but it may also enable you to undertake additional activities within the same overall budget.

The above examples are fairly straightforward. There are other types of decisions that are less easy and are part of the effectiveness debate. Take, for example, a media relations campaign. Mass mailings or e-mailings of press releases are relatively cheap, but they are of variable effect. Face-to-face interviews can be extremely effective, but are very costly in terms of time compared to mass mailings and you can only reach a very limited number of people. Somewhere in between there are highly targeted mailings, tailor-made to discrete sectors of the press. The same questions of effectiveness and efficiency have to be asked, and the answer will vary depending on the importance of the message and the audience group you are addressing.

Two vital questions need to be asked when looking at effectiveness and efficiency.

Can you get what you want by spending less money?

By thinking laterally it may be possible to achieve exactly the same objective for a fraction of the cost. Examples of this are use of piggy-back mailings. For instance, building societies and banks send out statements to customers, an ideal opportunity to include additional material.

How about joint ventures with complementary organisations or products? We are all familiar with the washing machine and washing powder link-ups. Then there is sponsorship. It may be possible for you to sponsor an activity that will give you opportunities to raise name awareness or undertake corporate hospitality at a fraction of the cost of putting on alternative activities that are totally funded by you.

At the other end of the spectrum is the other question on effectiveness.

Will spending a little more add a great deal of value?

Effectiveness does not mean looking to spend the least amount of money all the time; it means getting the most from your money. Sometimes, by spending a little more, a great deal of value can be added. Take a customer magazine. It could also be mailed out to selected press, to shareholders, to the company pensioners, just for the cost of a run-on of the print plus postage. The effect could be worth many times the extra cost.

It could be that holding a press conference on site and getting all the journalists there might be more costly, but it could be very much more effective, especially if there are visual elements involved like a new manufacturing process that is difficult to explain.

Equipment

It goes without saying that a programme or campaign cannot run effectively unless there is the right sort of equipment to support it. Public relations professionals do not require vast amounts of capital equipment, but it is important that it is up to date. Communication professionals need access to, and use of, technology appropriate to their needs. Video conferencing, use of the Internet and desktop publishing were all new technologies once, but they are now just a part of the battery of communication channels that can and should be used.

A note of caution should be sounded. When working on or with international programmes it is easy to assume that every country has ready access to new technologies. This is not the case. It is important therefore not to become wholly dependent on new technology.

In summary, when drawing together a budget these three factors must be borne in mind. An example of the main budget headings for a public relations programme is given below.

Budget headings

Human	Operating costs	Equipment
Staff salaries Employment costs (eg NI, pensions, benefits) Overheads and expenses (eg heat, light, office space)	Print and production Photography Media relations Conferences, seminars Sponsorship, etc Operating expenses (eg fax, telephone, stationery, post)	Office furniture Computer equipment and consumables Telephones, fax machines, etc

These costs are basically the same whether working in-house or in a consultancy. However, when employing consultancies the salaries element is obviously different. You will pay fees for the programme agreed upon.

These fees will normally be split into two sections.

Advisory fee

This covers consultancy advice, attending meetings, preparing reports, etc. This is usually based on a fixed amount of time per month or on a project basis.

Implementation fee

This covers the amount of executive time required to implement the agreed programme or campaign. For ongoing programmes this is again often based on a fixed amount of time per month, the idea being that some months more time will be devoted to the programme than others, but the work evens itself out in the end as far as payment is concerned. Some clients prefer to be billed for the actual amount of time spent, particularly if implementation includes a fair amount of project work that requires a variable amount of input from the consultancy.

You will often pay a 'mark-up' on bought-in services such as photography and print where the consultancy has a legal and financial responsibility for client work (the Public Relations Consultants Association (PRCA) recommends 17.65 per cent to cover things like indemnity insurance). You will usually have to pay value added tax (VAT) unless the consultancy is very small and not registered.

A typical monthly invoice from a consultancy might look as follows:

Invoice Headings

		£
PR	Executive time (35 hours at £65 per hour)	2275.00
	Photography (for product launch)	540.50
	Photography (for in-house magazine)	742.70
	Design and print for magazine	2450.00
	Design and print for schools pack	3820.00
PR	Operating expenses (fax, phone, stationery, post)	408.00
	Travel (day return to London and subsistence)	54.00
		10290.20
	VAT at 17.5%	1800.79
		12090.99

Overall budgets will be the subject of negotiation. There are, however, two main approaches to budgeting. The first is to adopt a formula approach that applies company-wide so as to determine the proportion of resources allocated to each function. Typical formulae that are applied are a percentage of the organisation's profits or sales turnover, a fixed increase on the first year's budget, or a sum comparable to that of the closest competitor. The main problem with this approach is that it takes no real account of the actual job of work that is required from public relations. The year ahead may involve a great deal of public relations input, for example if the organisation is to mount a major customer care campaign. The range of publics to be contacted varies from organisation to organisation. For some organisations, public relations as opposed to other forms of marketing communication may be the largest or even the only means of promotional activity.

An alternative approach is to start with the tasks that public relations needs to perform, cost them, and negotiate the budget on the basis of what is required. This does not give carte blanche to the public relations professional, since it is likely that each activity will be carefully scrutinised and will need to be justified. Wherever possible a cost:benefit analysis should be provided to support public relations expenditure. This entails you listing the costs of an activity on one side against the benefits obtained on the other. If a monetary value can be put against these benefits and they outweigh the costs, so much the better. It is also worth doing a reverse analysis and listing the negative costs of not undertaking the activity.

In most instances a mix of these two approaches is taken. Generally speaking an initial indication of the overall budget available will be given, the practitioner will then put together a detailed plan with costings attached, and the final budget will be negotiated.

Should the proposed budget prove unacceptable, some of the activities suggested will have to be cut or their scope narrowed. Inevitably compromises will have to be made; however, carefully detailed plans will demonstrate the consequences of cuts or indicate a list of essential core activities, as well as itemising the benefits of the full programme.

9

Knowing what you've achieved: evaluation and review

MEASURING SUCCESS

Public relations is no different from any other business function that you spend money on. You want to know if you are getting value for money. You need to know how effective you've been and if you've not been as effective as you thought you should have been, you need to discover why.

The first thing to do is define the terms. **Evaluation** is an ongoing process if you are talking about long-term programmes. Thus, you will regularly evaluate the media relations element of your programme by making a monthly critical analysis of your media coverage. As a result of this you may focus more effort on particular messages or journalists.

Similarly, at the end of a specific campaign, you will evaluate the results. So if the objective was to prevent the closure of a factory, you will have a clear-cut indication of the result at the end! You've either succeeded or failed.

Review applies to longer-term programmes. It would generally be extremely sensible to take a good, hard look at the programme each year. You will look at what the evaluation over the year has shown you, revisit the programme objectives and scrutinise the strategy. It could well be that you carry on as before, but it may be that you will want a complete reorientation of the programme. We will return to this later.

On shorter campaigns you might have to undertake a review if the strategy and tactics are clearly wrong because the campaign is not working.

In a nutshell, evaluation is both a monitoring and tweaking process and an analysis of the end results of a campaign or programme, while review is a periodic step back to identify any strategic changes that need to take place.

In 1999, the top 10 European consultancies earned £374 million[1] income. The top 10 UK consultancies earned £208 million[2] and the typical budget for in-house departments was about £530,000 per annum.[3]

It is no wonder then that clients and companies are keen to know what public relations is doing for them.

---

[1]Pawinska, M (2000) 'The Top European PR Consultancies 2000', *PR Week,* 23 June (owned groups and networks).
[2]'The Top 150 PR Consultancies', *PR Week,* 28 April 2000.
[3]Welch, Stephen (1999) 'In-house survey', *PR Week,* 18 August.

THE BENEFITS OF EVALUATION

It could be that evaluation is viewed as a great chore, best avoided if possible because it means that your head is on the block. But why shouldn't you be accountable? Most people are. Dishwashers are meant to produce clean dishes and advertising professionals are meant to generate sales; public relations professionals are not a privileged élite doing high and lofty things that are far too important or intangible to measure.

If undertaken properly, evaluation actually puts you in the driving seat. It helps you spot danger signs before real problems develop and it helps you prove your worth. Here are a few reasons why you should build evaluation into your campaigns and programmes:

- *It focuses effort.* If you know you are going to be measured on a number of key agreed targets, you will focus on the important and keep the secondary in perspective.
- *It demonstrates effectiveness.* There is no success like success! If you achieve what you have aimed to achieve, no one can take that from you. You can prove your worth.
- *It ensures cost efficiency.* Because you are concentrating on the things that should take priority, you will spend your budget and your time (which is also money) on the things that count and achieve the big results.
- *It encourages good management.* Management by objectives, having clear goals, brings sharpness to the whole public relations operation. The irrelevant will be quickly identified and rejected.
- *It facilitates accountability.* Not only your accountability to produce results, which is perfectly in order, but it also makes other people accountable in their dealings with you. You can quite legitimately say 'If I spend time doing this unscheduled project, it means that I cannot complete this planned activity. Which is more important?'

Then clear choices can be made about what may be new and pressing priorities. If the planned activity is also essential, then you might need extra help – so you are in a powerful position to ask for more people or extra budget.

WHY PRACTITIONERS DON'T EVALUATE

In a survey of IPR members' attitudes to evaluation, Tom Watson[1] discovered that many practitioners lacked confidence in promoting evaluation methods to clients and employees.

When questioned about their motives for undertaking evaluation, 'prove value of campaign/budget' came out a very clear leader, followed by 'help campaign targeting and planning' and 'need to judge campaign effects'. Another reason, 'help set more resources/fees', came a distant fourth.

Watson's research showed that practitioners were defensive about their activities. They used evaluation techniques to present data on which they could be judged rather than using evaluation to improve programmes.

The most used technique was providing an output measure for media relations (eg the range of publications in which coverage was obtained) rather than measuring the impact of the media relations campaign itself. Generally speaking, output measurement was seen to be more relevant than gauging impact or gaining intelligence so that programmes could be improved.

Watson also pinpointed the main reasons why programmes were not formally evaluated. These were, first, lack of knowledge (possibly disinclination to learn about evaluation techniques), second, 'cost', followed by 'lack of time' and 'lack of

---

[1]Quoted in Watson, T (1997) 'Measuring the success rate: Evaluating the PR process and PR programmes', in *Public Relations Principles and Practice*, ed P J Kitchen, International Thomson Business Press, London.

budget'. When added together, 'cost' and 'lack of budget' became the dominant reasons.

There are other reasons why evaluation is seen to be problematic.

- *Understanding what it is that has to be evaluated.* Often what is measured is output not outcome. So we will be very happy to see a nice, fat clippings file and will spend money to pay a clipping agency to collate the file for us. We may even do some more sophisticated form of analysis like trying to measure the worth of a clipping depending on its position on the page, its size, the number of key messages it contains and so on. There are several companies that provide such a service. Some will provide a more detailed analysis, for example, a breakdown of how many times specific publications or journalists used your press releases and the types of treatment your story received.

  However, in the long run it doesn't matter how heavy the clippings file is, what matters is what those clippings achieved (the outcome). As a result was there a 20 per cent increase in attendance at the AGM? Has the attitude of your key public altered?

- *Understanding what can be achieved.* Public relations practitioners should make realistic promises. It is just not possible to get the chief executive on the front page of the *Financial Times* every month unless he or she or the organisation is exceptional in some way (or notorious!). What is required is an honest, sober appraisal of what can be achieved. That knowledge comes with good research and the benefit of experience. Managing expectations is a key practitioner task.

  The over-promising problem is exacerbated by a genuine lack of knowledge of the psychological art of the possible. As detailed in Chapter 5 it is very difficult, or at least will require a very determined and fact-filled campaign, to convert people who have a fixed view to take on the opposite view. It is a less onerous task if the target public has no view at all, or it is reasonably well disposed because your message confirms or fits in with its own desires or views. Again research will identify audience attitudes and therefore the size of the public relations task.

- *Aggregation.* Sometimes it is difficult to identify precisely what the public relations' contribution was if there were other forms of communication activity, such as advertising, direct mail and special promotions.
- *Range of evaluation techniques required.* Public relations is unlike some other forms of marketing communication, such as direct mail, where the evaluation is relatively simple: you count the number of returns and the business transacted. Public relations addresses many audiences in many different ways and different types of evaluation technique are needed. So practitioners need to be aware of the different research techniques available and to have the resources necessary to undertake them.

More recently there have been a number of positive developments that have moved the evaluation agenda long and there are useful guides on the subject, such as the IPR- and PRCA-sponsored *The Public Relations Research and Evaluation Toolkit*,[1] which has helped to take some of the mystique and fear out of the subject.

It is impossible in this book to give an evaluation blueprint for every type of public relations activity. For some activities evaluation will be quite easy. If you are running an exhibition stand it is a simple, quantitative exercise to count the number of product enquiries, take

---

[1] Fairchild, M (1999) *The Public Relations Research and Evaluation Toolkit: How to measure the effectiveness of PR*, Institute of Public Relations and Public Relations Consultants Association with *PR Week*.

contact addresses and then trace back subsequent product orders.

Other things like the effects of a long-term sponsorship programme are much more difficult to evaluate.

PRINCIPLES OF EVALUATION

There are a number of principles of evaluation that help to set the context and make the task easier.

- *Objectives* are critical. Public relations campaigns can be seen to be effective when they achieve their objectives in a well-managed way. So objectives need to be achievable and measurable, and to ensure that they are you need to research and pre-test them wherever possible. 'Raising awareness' is not a good objective unless you quantify by how much (1 per cent or 99 per cent?) and with whom (define your public). Research will show you what is possible. Some objectives will be fairly simple to quantify. A campaign to change a law will either succeed or not, or it may be partially successful. There is also likely to be a set timeframe over which to work. A long-term campaign to change the general attitude towards the decriminalisation of drugs is likely to have patchy, incremental results over a long period. However, even in this situation it is possible to lay down clear benchmarks. For example, a legitimate objective would be to persuade the majority of chief constables by the year 2005, or give up the campaign.

  The achievement of objectives is the clearest way to evaluate any programme or campaign.
- *Evaluation* needs to be considered at the beginning of the process. It's too late to ask the question 'How did we do?' at the end if you didn't build in the mechanisms for measurement at the beginning.

- *Evaluation* is continuous. The decisions that have to be taken all along the communication chain affect the communication outcome. You have to decide on the message, the medium, the form of words and/or images, and ensure the target is receiving and interpreting the communication correctly. 'Evaluation' has to take place all along the chain. If one element is wrong, the desired outcome will be in jeopardy. Thus evaluation just at the end of a programme can be misleading.
- *Evaluation* must be objective and scientific. This means that public relations practitioners need to be proficient themselves or need to enlist the services of specialists who know about social scientific research and evaluation methods.
- *Evaluating* programmes and processes. Public relations programmes and campaigns require evaluating for the results of the communication activity, and also for their management. It is useful to separate out and list the achievements of your programme objectives (eg sponsorship achieved objective of 20 per cent awareness in target group) and the fact that you managed the campaign well (eg you did it at 10 per cent under budget).

There are a number of terms that are often used in evaluation that merit explanation. For each programme or campaign there will be:

- *Input*. This is what the public relations professional does and how these 'products' are distributed. For example, you might write, design and distribute an in-house journal. When evaluating inputs, elements such as the quality of the background research, writing, effectiveness of design and choice of distribution channels are measured.
- *Output*. This is how the inputs are used, either by the target public directly (eg how many employees read the journal) or by a third party who is a channel or opinion

former to the target public (eg how many newspapers printed your key messages?). So evaluation of outputs often involves counting and analysing things, for example, readership and circulation, media mentions and content analysis.

- *Outcome*. This involves measuring the end effect of the communication. How many employees who read the magazine took up the opportunity to join the local sports club at a reduced rate? Outcomes are measured in three ways:
  - changes at the thinking or awareness level (cognitive);
  - changes in the attitude or opinion level (affective);
  - changes in behaviour (conative).

This reflects the fact that objectives are set in these three ways (see Chapter 5). To measure them sometimes requires sophisticated research, including attitude surveys, focus groups and individual interviews. For some campaigns, however, measurement can be relatively easy, such as sales at the launch of a product (as the Lego Mindstorms example in Chapter 4 shows).

Thus it can be seen that if you want changes in opinion as the result of your campaign, this will be your objective, and to evaluate the programme you will need to measure opinions. It is not good enough to show newspaper cuttings that contain the message you wish to get across in order to change opinions. Media relations is a route by which you may achieve your end, and your success in this area is worth noting, but it is not your end result. Success in the media is an output, not an outcome.

- *Out-take*. This term is sometimes used to describe an intermediate position between an output and an outcome, and describes what an individual might extract from a communications programme, but it may or may not lead to further action that you can measure as a result. If a message in your house magazine is about discounted membership of the local sports club, you could measure how many employees actually remember that message, ie have extracted the relevant information from your article, but there is likely to be a difference between the number who demonstrate an out-take from the magazine and those who go on to sign up for membership.

AN EVALUATION MODEL AND SOME OTHER MEASURES

Putting together these evaluation principles it is possible to come up with an evaluation process that can be applied to most situations, but there is no gold standard for evaluation – individual programmes and campaigns need tailor-made evaluations.

A useful device is the macro model of evaluation demonstrated by Jim Macnamara[1] (see Figure 9.1). The model forms a pyramid. At the base are inputs, basically information and planning, and at the peak, objectives achieved. Each activity is split down into the various steps of the communication process. The model recognises inputs and asks the user to make a judgement on the quality of information, the choice of medium and the content of the communication. It then considers outputs, that is the communication produced, for example, the newsletter, the press release, the brochure, and then it considers the results or outcomes – what the communication actually achieved. Alongside the steps is a list of evaluation methods that might be used for a media campaign, a newsletter and so on.

The model needs to be customised for each project, but the basics remain the same. Its strength is that it recognises a range of evaluation methods; there is no all-embracing magic formula.

---

[1]Macnamara, J R (1992) 'Evaluation of public relations: The Achilles' heel of the PR profession', *International Public Relations Review*, vol 15, November.

The more advanced evaluation methods further up the pyramid, which measure outcomes, are recommended. They are more sophisticated and of course more expensive. The ones lower down the pyramid are more basic and can be seen as tests that you are doing things right, more akin to quality control. However, these basic checks are not to be missed. You can be more confident of success higher up the pyramid if you get the basics right.

In practical terms how does this translate into reality? Here is a checklist of critical factors to consider when planning a campaign or programme:

- set measurable objectives;
- build in evaluation and quality checks from the start;
- agree measurement criteria with whoever will be judging the success of your work;
- establish monitoring procedures that are open and transparent, for example, monthly reviews of progress;
- demonstrate results.

Objective evaluation measures

Typical objective measures that might be employed are:

- changes in behaviour, (if a product is given public relations support, buyer behaviour can be tracked);
- responses (return of reply-paids, response slips, salesforce quotes, etc);
- changes in attitude, opinion and awareness – especially important for opinion-former work (can be measured through telephone research, questionnaires, one-to-one interviews);
- achievements (80 per cent of retailers came to promotional conference);
- media coverage, content, distribution, readership, share of voice (content analysis, readership data);
- budget control and value for money (a process measure).

EVALUATION OF PUBLIC RELATIONS PROGRAMME

STAGES	ACTIVITIES	METHODOLOGIES
RESULTS	Objective achieved or problem solved	• Observation (in some cases) • Quantitative research
	Number who behave in a desired manner	• Sales statistics, enrolments etc • Quantitative research • Qualitative research (cognition acceptance)
	Number who change attitudes	• Qualitative research
	Number who learn message content (eg increased knowledge, awareness, understanding)	• Readership, listenership or viewership statistics • Attendance at events • Inquiry or response rates (eg coupons, calls)
	Number who consider messages	• Circulation figures • Audience analysis
	Number who receive messages	
	Number of messages supporting objectives	• Analysis of media coverage (Breakdown positive, negative and netural – eg Media Content Analysis)
OUTPUTS	Number of messages placed in the media	• Media monitoring (clippings and broadcast media tapes) • Distribution statistics
	Number of messages sent	• Expert review • Audience surveys • Feedback • Awards
	Quality of message presentation (eg newsletter or brochure design, newsworthiness of story)	• Readability tests (eg Gunning, Flesch, SST) • Review • Pre-testing (eg focus groups)
INPUTS	Appropriateness of message content	
	Appropriateness of the medium	• Case studies • Pre-testing
	Adequacy of background information, intelligence, research	• Review • Benchmark

Figure 9.1 *Macnamara's macro model of evaluation*

It is sometimes relatively easy to put in checks when measuring the effectiveness of editorial, if you work in conjunction with other marketing colleagues. For example, when the author worked in-house for a large building society, she was able to place some editorial material next to a financial product advert that had been running for a few weeks in the *Sunday Times*. The number of policies that came from the two adverts previous to the editorial were 27 and 21 respectively. The advert with adjacent editorial resulted in 94 policies being sold from coupons.

Similarly, for another financial product it was found that adjacent editorial doubled the coupon returns from a series of adverts in the *Sunday Telegraph*.

There are examples of how the effectiveness of campaigns can be measured in the case studies in Chapter 7.

Subjective evaluation measures

Apart from quantitative objective measures, subjective measures of performance are also quite legitimate. They are the icing on the cake and often put the fun into working in what are often the quite stressful conditions of day-to-day public relations life. These factors may be especially important in the client/consultancy relationship, but are also highly prized in the relationships that in-house departments build with other departments within their organisation. In fact what often wins business for consultancies (all things being equal) and ready co-operation from other departments are these subjective yardsticks.

- enthusiasm;
- efficiency and professionalism;
- creativity;
- initiative;
- an instinct for what is right in a given situation (based on judgement gained through experience);
- people chemistry.

Evaluating the process

A critical part of evaluation is to monitor the process. Part of this is the effective deployment of both staff and budgets. Regular, rigorous monitoring of both is required.

Staff need to be continuously developed to cope with and exploit the rapidly changing communication environment. It is also essential that public relations staff are well motivated and well directed. They are, after all, the handlers and managers of the organisation's reputation in a most overt sense. If they do not believe in what they are doing, how can they do their job proficiently and professionally?

Likewise, the management and effective use of budgets is a duty laid on every manager, including the public relations professional. With so many options open on how to spend what is often quite a limited budget, he or she must have a keen regard to the careful stewardship of resources. Every pound should count. Chapter 8 gives a more detailed exposition on how budgeting can be done effectively.

MEDIA ANALYSIS

Having said that media analysis is a measure of output rather than outcome, it is very significant. In fact, a survey of UK in-house practitioners[1] showed that 19 per cent of total budgets were spent on media relations, with increasing amounts of additional activity being carried out on an outsourcing basis by external agencies. So it is vital that these campaigns are seen to be delivering at the output level. The following case study illustrates the point.

Why media analysis is good news for IBM

How does a global corporation keep track of the so-called 'thud-factor' – the many hundreds of press articles

---

[1]Pawinsta, M (1999) 'In-house PR survey', *PR Week*, 20 August.

that portray them in a good, indifferent or bad light? For a truly international company like IBM, which has customers in every country in the world, monitoring the media is not just a useful practice for its internal communications teams, it is a vital business measurement tool for senior management.

IBM employs the services of a specialist media analysis firm to provide detailed information on every media mention about the company, its financial performance, its brand, its products and its services. In this way, a clear and precise picture can be built up showing what has been reported, where it appeared, how it was presented, who wrote it and, most importantly, whom it might influence and in what way.

Media analysis for IBM is a complex exercise. Not only are there many different product and service areas to monitor and analyse, but the company operates in many countries and across various industry sectors. The list of media outlets regularly carrying reports about IBM runs into thousands, which are monitored, clipped and analysed as part of the evaluation process.

Echo Research, an international media analysis and communications research company, works for IBM Global Industries, which is made up of separate business areas targeting different customer sectors with IBM's e-business messages. One of these is the European Finance Sector, which average about 150 cuttings each month, in publications that are read by decision-makers in major banks, investment companies and other financial institutions.

Cultural differences and language barriers, combined with the vast differences in how the media operate from country to country, were the key drivers behind IBM's decision to appoint a PR agency in each country. Gradually, a network of agencies was established, covering 11 countries in the European Finance Sector – Belgium, Denmark, France, Germany, Italy, The Netherlands, Spain, Sweden, Switzerland, Turkey and the United Kingdom. The role of the agencies was to focus on building awareness of IBM in the business and trade media, rather than in the IT and technology journals where IBM was always high on the news agenda. The goal was to be the talk of the vertical markets in which IBM was most interested in building its business, relying on the media in each country to spread the news about the positive benefits of various IBM products and services.

Echo's media evaluation is an IT-based system, which is used to capture media issues and messages coded by trained research analysts, perform analysis of the data, and generate data reports and charts for inclusion in client reports. The way the data is relayed back to each individual client varies, depending on how it is to be used or disseminated internally. For IBM Global Industries, Echo provides quarterly reports comprising a summary report and analysis combined with a full run of data relating to the previous quarter. The summary report is posted on to an internal Intranet, making it universally available to various departments and employees within IBM. It provides senior managers with an overview of what the media are saying, covering highlights for the quarter, lead topics, key messages and issues in specific publications/ markets, and ratings, together with conclusions and recommendations. This is supported by a full run of data that shows detailed ratings on the quality of the coverage. The number of headings under which articles are evaluated include position, origin, descriptors associated with IBM, issues raised, whether competitors were mentioned, and the presence and strength of messages carried.

According to Keith Gold, Director of the Finance Sector of IBM Global Industries, 'Media evaluation is absolutely central to our communications process. We can move fast to adapt our strategy if necessary, pick up on emerging issues, and identify trends and respond accordingly.'

REVIEWING THE SITUATION

While evaluation takes place on an ongoing basis, a thorough review takes place less often. As explained earlier (Chapter 4), a major review including extensive research may well take place before a programme or campaign is put in place. That will entail a close examination and analysis of both the external and internal environments, as well as all the aspects of constructing a viable plan outlined in this book.

Again, all good managers undertake a regular review of their programmes. A look every 3 months and a longer look every 12 months ensures that everything is on track, and that any new situations are taken into account. Minor modifications can be made as the programme progresses.

The annual review will need to be tough and may involve examining new or ongoing research. A day or couple of days away from the office with colleagues who are working with you is time well spent to ensure that all is in order.

There are, however, a number of external and internal 'drivers' that might force a review of a programme or campaign, or indeed its complete abandonment in mid-stream.

While it is essential to tweak tactics as a plan unfolds, especially in the light of information that ongoing evaluation brings, the plan itself should remain as the route-map, with some flexibility to accommodate opportunities and problems as they arise. That is because the objectives remain the same and the strategy holds good. However, it is essential to bear in mind that public relations is conducted within a dynamic environment and there must be the capability to respond as soon as possible, either in a proactive way to lead or forestall events, or in a reactive way to deal with an emergency situation. A review is required if the overall objectives need to be changed or if the strategy is seen not to be working. Let's deal with the strategy issues first.

HELP, THE STRATEGY'S NOT WORKING!

If the underlying strategy for a programme or campaign turns out to be wrong, this is a very serious business. To get the strategy wrong indicates fundamental flaws in research or the interpretation of research. An example will illustrate. Suppose a company wants to launch a new product and the public relations strategy is to mount a media relations campaign including a press launch with product demonstrations, merchandising packs for the regional and consumer press, competitions, consumer offers and a couple of stunts designed to attract attention.

Suppose after all this, the product doesn't sell at all well. There are a number of explanations and here are just a few!:

- The product is sub-standard. As soon as the public relations professional becomes aware of this the company must be advised accordingly. If the company insists on going ahead, at least it was told. The public relations professional may resign over such an issue. The damage to long-term reputation could be severe.
- The product is a 'me too' and has no distinguishing features. No amount of good public relations will persuade people to buy this type of product rather than their current favourite, unless of course there are brand strengths. Public relations should not over-promise.
- The product and the message are aimed at the wrong target markets. There is a major flaw in research.
- The message is not accepted. It could be you're saying the wrong things, or in the wrong way, or that the medium or the timing is wrong. There is lack of research or misinterpretation of information.
- The product needs to be sampled by consumers for them to really appreciate it. Then why choose media relations as your main communications vehicle?
- The press aren't interested. You haven't found the right media hook: you aren't approaching them in the right way. It could be lack of research. Maybe another big

179

consumer story is breaking at the same time as your launch. Oh dear! Sometimes all the market intelligence and research in the world can't protect you from this nightmare. In this case your strategy may even be right, but you'll have to change either that or your tactics quickly to get back on the front foot again. Creativity counts.

If the strategy is not working you need to ask two questions:

- *Are my objectives right and realisable?* If the answer to that is 'no' then no wonder the strategy's not working. If the answer is 'yes' then the second question is necessary.
- *What's wrong with the strategy?* What basic point have I overlooked or misinterpreted? This means a return to the research, and a careful analysis. Did you ask the right questions in the first place? Did you ask them all? What do the unanswered questions really tell you? Do you really understand your publics and what can be achieved? Do your messages have credibility and can they be delivered via the tactics you have plumped for? Is the programme too ambitious or perhaps not sufficiently ambitious? Is the programme adequately resourced?

It is embarrassing to say the least to get the strategy wrong but, if you've done careful research and are confident of your interpretation, it is likely that the tactics, not the strategy, needs correcting. However, as with all things, it is better to admit when something is wrong and correct it, rather than limp along wasting time and resources, and damaging your professional reputation.

EXTERNAL AND INTERNAL REVIEW DRIVERS

Through the regular evaluation and review process, adjustments will be made to your campaign or programme.

Objectives might be refocused or given a different priority and tactics may be altered. This is part of being effective and in tune with changing requirements. Minor ongoing changes can be expected. However, all the best-laid plans are subject to major review or even reversal if fundamental changes in the external or internal environment call for it. Thankfully these 'drivers' occur relatively infrequently, but it is wise to have contingency plans ready to deal with them if or when they do arise, because they usually require some pretty fast-footed action and you may only have one shot at getting it right.

The list below gives a flavour of the sort of external drivers that could force a review:

- legislative change that either threatens or gives expanded opportunities to the organisation;
- competitor activity, which threatens or gives opportunity;
- takeover or acquisition (note, if a company is taken over through a hostile bid it then has to switch its public relations endeavour from actively campaigning against the acquirers to working for them);
- major product recall or damage to corporate reputation;
- action by a well-organised, powerful, opposing pressure group.

Internal drivers can also make a review essential. The kinds of scenarios that would force this are:

- corporate restructure with new priorities, which may entail the splitting up or restructuring of the public relations function;
- changes in key personnel such as the chief executive (or the director of public relations!);
- budget changes, meaning that public relations activity is significantly cut or expanded;
- future needs. A programme or campaign may end or run out of steam. A fresh look is then required to reactivate and refocus the public relations work.

Once having decided on a review, the planning process then begins its cycle again. Figure 3.2 on page 41 outlines the process. Again the basic questions have to be addressed:

- What are you trying to achieve?
- Who do you want to reach?
- What do you want to say?
- What are the most effective ways of getting the message across?
- How can success be measured?

By systematically working through these questions, all the essentials of planning and managing a successful public relations programme will be covered.

AND FINALLY!

This book has given you the basic framework for putting together a well-founded public relations campaign.

Careful, systematic planning will make your life so much easier. Add one more vital ingredient – flair, the ability to think outside the square, and your work in public relations will be immensely rewarding. There is nothing more exciting than seeing a communication programme buzz and take on a life that can only come from the sort of work the public relations professional does. Communication is about making contact, developing relationships, building trust and achieving results which add to the success of your organisation because the key stakeholders support you. Careful planning and management lies at the heart of that.

Good planning and good luck!

Index

active publics 105
advisory fees 159
AIDA model 91–92
all issue publics 105
analysis 43, 48–77
apathetic publics 106
'appropriateness of tactics' test 122–24
attitude formation 79–80
'attitude' objectives 93
'Attrition by Charm' campaign 135–39
aware publics 105
'awareness' objectives 93

'behaviour' objectives 93
boundary-spanning role of PR 7–8
budgeting 159, 160–61
business role of PR 5–7

communication audit 67–68
communication managers and technicians 17–19
communication models 81–87
communication role of PR 7–11
Compaq Computers campaign 73–77
constraint recognition 107
constraints on objectives 97–98
consultancy fees 159–60
context, PR in 20–33
contingency planning 144–46
continuous research 61
'convergence' model of communication 83, 84
co-orientation model of group communication 85
costs see resources
crisis management 144–46
critical path analysis 149–50, 151, 153

'decline' stage of businesses 28
'deliverability of tactics' test 124
Domino Theory of communication 91

EPISTLE analysis 50
equipment 158
evaluation 162–77
expert prescribers 18
external review drivers 180–82

fees, consultancy 159–60
Firefly Communications 73–77
Fishburn Hedges 129–35
flexibility of plans 45–47, 120–21
focus groups 65
function-oriented structures 16

groups, communicating with 84–85
'growth' stage of businesses 26–27

Harry Ramsden's restaurant campaign 125–29
hot-issue publics 105–06
human resources 155–56

IBM Global Industries 175–77
IFA Promotion campaign 140–43
implementation fees 159–60
informal research 66
'input' definition 169
intelligence gathering 7–10
internal review drivers 180–82
Internet communication 87–90
Internet groups 65–66
interpretation of data 68
interviews 63–65
'involvement level' factors 107
issues management 30–31, 53–56

Lansons Communications 140–43

latent publics   105
Lego Mindstorms campaign   69–73, 94
long-term programmes   139–43, 150–52, 154

Macnamara's model of evaluation 171–74
manager roles   17–19
Manning, Selvage and Lee campaign 70–73, 94
mass audiences, communicating with 85–87
'maturity' stage of businesses   27–28
media analysis   175–77
media influence on public opinion 109
media relations function   18
media research   66–67
messages   112–16
Mindstorms campaign   69–73
models of communication   81–87
models of evaluation   171–75
models of planning   40–42
'monitoring public opinion' role 9–10

'Night at the Opera' campaign 125–29
non-publics   104–05

objective-setting   43, 45, 78–99, 168
one-off research   61–62
operating costs   156–58
organisational characteristics   28–30
organisational development stages 25–28
organisational structure of PR   14–17
organisations, role of PR within 7–14
'output', 'outcomes' and 'out-takes' 169–71

people as an expandable resource 5–6
PEST analysis   49–53
Pilkington PLC   37–39
policy statements   37–39
'Power to the Pre-Schools' campaign 129–35

Pre-School Learning Alliance campaign   129–35
primary research   62–63
private sector contexts   24–25
problem recognition   106–07
problem-solving process facilitators 18
public opinion   31–32, 101–04
public relations definitions   2–3
public sector contexts   24
publics   21–23, 100–12

questionnaires   63
questions, basic planning   39–42

'receivers' of information   91–93
reputation management, PR as   3–4
research see analysis; context
researchers   60–61
resources   33, 155–61
review   163, 178
Royal Irish Regiment campaign 135–39

secondary research   62
sectoral considerations   24–25
Shandwick International   125–29
single issue publics   105
stages of planning process   43–47
stakeholder analysis   57–59
starting planning processes   34–47
'start-up' business development stage 26
status of PR   12–14, 15
strategic objectives   98–99
strategic role of PR   8–9, 12
strategy stage of PR planning 117–21, 179–80
SWOT analysis   56–57

tactical objectives   98–99
tactics   119–39
task-oriented structures   14–16
technician roles   17, 18–19
telephone interviews   64–65
timescales   32, 147–54
two-step communication model   86

Wallace Connections   129–35